Making Your Point

▶ A Process Approach to Argumentation

Linda Watkins-Goffman
Hostos Community College,
City University of New York

Richard W. Goffman

Clara W. Velazquez
Hostos Community College,
City University of New York

NEWBURY HOUSE

Heinle & Heinle Publishers
A Division of Wadsworth, Inc.
Boston, Massachusetts 02116 U.S.A.

The publication of *Making Your Point* was directed by the members of the Heinle & Heinle ESL Publishing Team:

Erik Gundersen, Editorial Director
Susan Mraz, Marketing Manager
Kristin Thalheimer, Production Editor

Also participating in the publication of this program were:

Publisher: Stanley J. Galek
Editorial Production Manager: Elizabeth Holthaus
Associate Editor: Lynne Telson Barsky
Project Manager: Judy Keith
Manufacturing Coordinator: Mary Beth Lynch
Photo Coordinator: Carl Spector
Interior Designer: Christine Reynolds
Cover Illustrator: Viqui Maggio
Cover Designer: Robert Freese

ISBN: 0-8384-3404-5

Heinle & Heinle Publishers is a division of Wadsworth, Inc.

Manufactured in the United States of America.

10 9 8 7 6 5 4 3 2 1

CONTENTS

CHAPTER THREE—Bilingual Education: Help or Hindrance?

CHAPTER FOUR—Sexism: Inequality in the Workplace

CHAPTER FIVE—Right to Life? Right to Choose?

PREFACE

Making Your Point is the first advanced level expository writing text to focus exclusively on the mode of argumentation. In addition to giving extensive practice designed to develop students' argumentative writing, *Making Your Point* teaches the error analysis and latter stage second language acquisition editing skills necessary for the academic success of international students.

Since many students at the higher levels of English-as-a-Second-Language writing are capable of comprehending sophisticated texts, we have included provocative, exciting writings focusing on a variety of social issues, as well as suggested videotapes of movies related to the topics. Although vocabulary exercises are provided, the students are encouraged to read for meaning, and to mine for ideas they can use when they write their own compositions. Once they have written the first draft, students are led through the revising and editing processes, including exercises in argument writing and error analysis.

This book's predecessor, *Thinking To Write,* has provided students with a thorough introduction to each of the four rhetorical modes, starting with narration, progressing through description, and ending with argumentation and research. Having learned to incorporate the various modes into their argument writing, students can progress naturally to a more thorough investigation of this mode with *Making Your Point.* A chief goal of this text is to provide opportunities to practice writing to the "time, topic, and audience constraints," which will help students take timed essay exams successfully.

Though many advanced level international students can write relatively fluently in their second language, they frequently make errors in syntax and punctuation that impede their progress. In fact, it is often the case that a student who can write with facility on a complex issue will fail to catch many simple mistakes, such as subject-verb agreement errors or incorrect preposition use. For this reason, we have included grammar exercises both in the chapters themselves and in the Appendices, to help the students learn error analysis skills and become careful editors of their compositions.

Making Your Point could not have been written without the assistance of some special people, the most notable of whom are the students in our classes at Eugenio Maria de Hostos Community College of the City University of New York. We thank them for contributing comments, questions, and ideas for student drafts in this book. We would also like to thank Dr. Victor Cummings, Director of ESL at Hostos; Dr. Alfredo Villanueva, Chairperson of the English Department; Erik Gundersen, Editor, Intenstive/College ESL; and Lynne Telson Barsky, Associate Editor at Heinle & Heinle.

INTRODUCTION

This book focuses on a particular type of writing: argumentation, or "writing to convince." This is what you do when you want to communicate an idea, particularly an opinion, and convince your reader that your opinion is correct. Argument writing is a very useful skill that you will use again and again throughout your life, especially in certain career areas, such as business or law. Needless to say, you will certainly be asked to write persuasively throughout your educational career. Writing an essay in which you are asked to agree or disagree, and tell why, is often required in English courses, as well as in almost every other area of study.

This text is called ***Making Your Point***. Making your point, of course, means more than simply stating your opinion. After much talking, reading, thinking, and rethinking about an issue, you will discover what your opinion is on a particular topic. At that point you must learn to put your point across to your reader *persuasively*. In order to do this, you must first *state it clearly*; then *back it up* with thoughts and ideas that will convince the reader that your opinion has merit. This means that the *organization* of your essay is important.

Argument writing has various styles in different cultures and languages. American English argumentation requires you to be concise, clear, and organized in a straightforward, linear fashion, unlike in certain other languages. If your writing background is in another language or from another culture, this may be a change from what you are used to. (This is not meant to imply that the American style of expression is better or worse than any other. It simply is the one we are addressing here.) Noticing the differences and similarities between your native language or culture and English—and analyzing them—will be helpful to you in making the transition.

Writing is a creative process. It begins when you first start thinking about a topic, and ends when you finish the final copy. It is a creative, sometimes chaotic activity, in which the writer often discovers what he or she is trying to say during the actual process of writing. When we write, we are engaged in a thinking-on-paper process that begins with **prewriting**, progresses to writing the piece in a rough form (**drafting**), then continues through the rethinking or **revising** phase. The final step is **editing**, in which the draft is checked for errors in usage, spelling, and punctuation. After these errors are corrected, the final copy is complete. In this Introduction we will discuss what these stages of the composing process mean and how you will be encouraged to develop your own writing process in *Making Your Point*.

▶Prewriting

This stage includes any activity you do in order to start writing the composition. It may include freely discussing the topic in a group (sometimes called "brainstorming"), making a list, or drawing a diagram or chart. It may also include reading about the topic. Each chapter in this book includes a selection from a major newspaper or magazine on a controversial topic. The selections are intended both to model effective argument writing, as well as to cause the reader to agree or disagree. Your opinions, elicited by the selections, should form the basis for your own argument writing. Each chapter has questions or activities in the *Prewriting* section that will help you get started writing on the topic. In addition, you may be able to design your own prewriting activities.

EXERCISE 1: Introducing Yourself

You will often be working in groups or pairs while using this book in order to give and receive feedback, so it is important to get to know the other people who will be in your writing group. In order to introduce yourself to your classmates, write down in a list the facts about yourself that you want to share. This will serve as a prewriting exercise, for the purpose of writing a brief, self-introductory composition. (*Note*: This is the one and only time in this book when you are asked to write a composition that is *not* an argument essay.)

▶Writing the Draft

This part of the process is the actual writing of the composition in its roughest form. You should be concerned with communicating *what* you want to say to the reader. Getting your ideas across in a way that makes sense to the person who will read your draft is crucial at this stage.

When writing an argument paper in English, there is a general form or organization that is considered most acceptable. When you become more proficient at argument writing and more confident in your skills, you may want to vary the form. Until then, however, and for the purpose of this book, we will strive to perfect an efficient, direct, and economical style.

1. **Introduction**—This should include a clear and concise main idea or thesis. There should be no doubt in the reader's mind about what is to follow. This is no place for digression or subtlety. The main point of the composition—that is, the idea that you are trying to convince your reader to accept—should come through loudly and clearly.
2. **Body**—This part should be two or more supporting paragraphs that give evidence to back up what was written in the introductory paragraph. Your job here is to prove, with words, the truth of what you asserted in your introduction. To do this, you will present logical evidence. This evidence may be factual or anecdotal, and should be clearly connected to your main thesis. When you have access to factual evidence that you can document (that is, make reference to its source), use it. When you are writing an argument essay and have no such factual evidence, it is acceptable to use anecdotal evidence, such as ordinary examples from your own experience or observations of life.

   When you state your argument, you should show that you are not using a totally emotional rationale. A good way to take an intellectual approach to argument is by showing that you are familiar with the opposite point of view, stating the opposite point of view, and explaining why it is incorrect. In some cases you may very well have an emotional bias; if you do, it is acceptable to write your essay from this point of view, but you must say so near the beginning of the composition. Carefully explain the roots of your feelings. A carefully thought out argument which takes into account personal bias is more convincing to the reader than an emotional outpouring of words.

   In American English it is considered appropriate to use the first person singular when the writer is discussing his or her own point of view. It lends authenticity to the ideas presented in the essay. In some other cultures this is considered poor style. You may want to compare this aspect of discourse style of your native language with that of English.

3. **Conclusion**—This is usually contained in the last paragraph. It should reflect and summarize the content of your argument. It can be a restatement, including a reflection, analysis, or synthesis. It may also raise questions left unanswered that might be the focus of future discourse. The conclusion should make clear to the reader or audience that the composition is ending.

EXERCISE 2: Writing the Draft

After reviewing the list you wrote in Exercise 1, write a draft introducing yourself to the writing group. Try to convince the group that you will be a valuable member, and tell why. Follow the format we have just discussed, by including the three parts: Introduction, Body, and Conclusion.

▶Revising

After the first draft (or rough draft) is written, it is time to revise, because almost no writer, professional or amateur, experienced or beginner, can produce a perfect first draft. In order to improve upon a draft (or anything else), you must examine it closely, and analyze it to find its imperfections and weaknesses.

Of course, it is easier to analyze something done by someone else than something done by yourself, especially if you have just finished doing it. This is one of the reasons for having a writing group or writing partner—each person can help the other by looking at the work that has just been done with "fresh" or objective eyes and ears. Once you get some experience analyzing one another's drafts and finding ways to improve them, you will develop the ability to do the same thing with your own work.

One technique that is most helpful is to read your draft aloud to someone. Listen to how it sounds, see how it looks. You and the other readers should consider the ideas you have written, and ask basic questions about them, such as:

1. Is the writing clear and easily understood?
2. What is the writer's purpose? Is this purpose made clear?

3. Is the composition interesting? Is it boring? If it's boring, what specifics could be used to make it more interesting?
4. Are there parts that could have been left out? That is, are there sentences included that do little or nothing to advance the purpose of the composition?
5. Are there things left out which ought to have been included? Where? Are there some things mentioned that the reader would like to hear more about?

These are just some of the questions you should apply to all writing when analyzing it for revision. Each chapter of this book has a *Revising* section that offers suggested questions to help you change and improve your drafts. You may want to make major changes: you might add more information, or delete some irrelevant ideas. You could also change the order in which the ideas are presented. *In fact, you may want to start over from scratch with a whole new composition.* This, too, is revising, and a perfectly normal part of the writing process. At this stage, considering your peers' and the instructor's ideas is an important step toward improving your draft.

An important fact to remember to promote the smooth working of a writing group or writing partnership: When you comment on someone's draft, be sure to include at least one encouraging question or statement. No one likes to hear only negative criticism; almost every draft contains *some idea* worth praise.

At the revising stage, leave the grammar, spelling, and punctuation errors aside. You can deal with these errors after you have given consideration to the ideas.

Of particular interest at the revising stage of argument writing is *coherence.* Remember that your argument, in order to sound like native English, must flow from one idea to the next in a logical sequence. In the *Revising* section of each chapter we have included questions which deal with the interconnecting of ideas both from sentence to sentence and from paragraph to paragraph. You will learn how to use certain types of words that facilitate the interconnection of ideas. This will help to insure that your essays are coherent.

EXERCISE 3: Revising the Draft

Now take your draft and read it aloud to your group or partner. Listen to how it sounds, and ask your partner to make suggestions to improve the composition. Look over the Revising questions on pages xii–xiii and apply them to the composition.

Now, making the changes that seem to be most appropriate, revise your draft.

EXERCISE 4: Supporting Your Argument—Working Together

Following is a framework for an argument essay that tries to convince the reader that cats are better pets than dogs. You are given paragraph 1, the introduction, and paragraph 6, the conclusion.

1. Divide into four groups. Each group should select a paragraph to complete. Write the supporting paragraphs 2, 3, 4, and 5. Suggestions are given for specific areas you might cover in those paragraphs. You can use them or not; what is important is that you create supporting paragraphs that back up paragraph 1, and allow you to finish with paragraph 6, which confidently states that the point has been made.
2. Now, share what you have written in your groups. Choose one representative paragraph from each group and share it with the class either by writing it on the chalkboard or reading it aloud.

Cats Are Better Pets Than Dogs

1. [introduction] People keep pets of every kind, from hamsters and mice to horses and llamas, but the best pet of all is a cat. And certainly, compared to dogs, cats are far superior as companions and friends for human beings.

2. [first supporting paragraph: intelligence]

3. [second supporting paragraph: cleanliness, convenience, ease of care]

4. [third supporting paragraph: beauty, playfulness, positive effect on owner]

5. [fourth supporting paragraph: anecdotes about cats you have known]

6. [conclusion] Clearly you can see, for all the reasons I have just stated, there can be no doubt that cats have dogs beat in every possible way as the most wonderful pet a person can have!

At the end of each chapter's *Revising* section you will find a paragraph called "Screening Room." Under this heading we have made a suggestion for a film that is available on video and that you may find interesting to rent and watch as it relates to the topic covered in the reading selection of each chapter. You will be asked to write a reaction to the film, and to find ideas in it relevant to your topic.

▶Editing

If you think that the words "revising" and "editing" mean approximately the same thing, you are mistaken. Put simply, revising is about *ideas*; editing is about *form*. You have finished revising when you are satisfied that the ideas you want to communicate are being communicated. (This may include rewriting your composition one, two, or more times.) Now comes the time to take a look at the aspects of writing that we set aside earlier, the part that has to do with the *mechanics*, not the ideas, of communication. This is the fine-tuning of your writing, the final preparation for evaluation. This is the time to reread the draft, paying attention to and looking for errors in spelling, grammatical forms, and punctuation, identifying such errors, and correcting them.

Each chapter of this book has an *Editing* section that will help you focus on these kinds of errors. In addition, there are Appendices in the back of this text that give extra editing practice.

EXERCISE 5: Editing

Exchange your introductory essay with a writing partner. Edit the draft with a particular eye toward complete, non-run-on sentences. If sentence structure happens to be an area of writing weakness for you, circle each sentence in your composition so that you can focus on each one individually.

Apply the following five questions to each sentence in the essay you are editing.

1. Reading it over, is there any doubt in your mind about where each sentence begins and ends?
2. Does each sentence begin with a capital letter?
3. Does each sentence end with appropriate punctuation?
4. Does each sentence contain a subject and a verb?

5. Does each sentence express a complete thought, so that it could stand alone without the support of the sentences before and after it?

Was the answer to any of the questions "no"? If so, the writer must address those weaknesses and fix them. The writer needs to satisfy his or her "editor" that there aren't any questionable sentence structures in the composition.

The *Editing* section of each chapter includes grammar exercises to help you learn the rules of English syntax.

For many writers, prewriting, drafting, revising, and editing are not separate stages, but interrelated and overlapping. Some people revise and edit at the same time. Some write many drafts, others few. Realize that the thinking/writing process is idiosyncratic and individual: *no two writers are the same*. Use this book in any way that helps you, as long as you-as-writer understand the importance of both ideas and form, and their significance for the final product.

▶Writing with Time, Topic, and Audience Constraints

In each chapter there is an exercise designed to deal with the need for students to practice writing within the constraints of a specific time limit (for instance, writing a timed expository composition for college placement), a specific audience (for instance, a college professor), and a specific topic (for instance, a response to a leading question on an essay test). This section is an important component, because while the composing process helps you better understand yourself as a writer, it takes time. College students are often asked to write on demand. Many need practice in order to be comfortable writing, for instance, an in-class composition final, in which prewriting, drafting, revising, and editing must be done quickly within a single class period.

EXERCISE 6: Writing a Timed Essay

Write a draft in 30 minutes on the following topic: "Is Television Good or Bad for Children?" Assume that the people reading it will be a group of young, first-time parents.

For the time being, do not worry about neatness, spelling, or errors; there will be time to focus on these later. Right now, see if you can write your ideas down quickly in essay format.

Student essay sample

Each chapter of this book offers at least one actual student essay, written by a student in response to exercises like the ones that you are being asked to do. None of them is perfect; some are better than others. You will be asked to read and evaluate these essays, just as you must read and evaluate the essays written by members of your writing group, and as you must learn to do with your own written work.

EXERCISE 7: Evaluating a Student Essay

1. The student argument essay below was written in response to the question: "Is television bad for children?" Read it carefully.
2. Divide into groups. Using the Revising questions on pages xii–xiii and Editing questions on page xvi, evaluate it as if it were written by one of your classmates.
3. Each group should identify the introduction, body, and conclusion of the essay. Do you think that the composition is a good example of an argument essay, based on our discussion of argumentation so far? How does it compare with the draft you just wrote in the preceding exercise?

Television: Is It a Good or Bad Invention?

1 Almost every American family owns a television. They enjoy a variety of movies, news programs, and variety shows. Having a television means that we do not have to leave home in order to be entertained. This leads to a more economical lifestyle in a time of rising inflation and recession.

2 Besides entertainment, television offers a variety of educational shows for children and young people. For example, seeing a classic literary work transformed to film can encourage more reading of classics and science programs can encourage developing interests in the sciences. In the same way, a program about animals can be coupled with a trip to the zoo.

3 Unfortunately, parents sometimes misuse television and put it in the role of a babysitter, thinking that while the children's minds are engaged watching a program, they will not misbehave. For this reason, parents who are hard pressed for someone to mind

the children leave them watching television far too long. These children do not learn to read, play games, or relate to other children interactively.

4 In addition, children, if left unsupervised, watch programs which are inappropriate. Violent shows or sexually explicit material or programs glorifying inappropriate stereotypes as role models can harm children's very impressionable minds. One example of a tragic result of this situation comes to mind: a news story in Texas reported a child, a three-year old toddler, who had seen too many stories about Superman, thought he could fly. He jumped from an apartment window many floors up to his death below because he thought he was "Superman." This incident teaches us that we should discuss with the children what they watch and make sure they understand the difference between fact and fantasy, and that we should make sure the material is appropriate for the child's age level.

5 So it seems that television can be either good or bad depending on who is using it and how it is used. Particularly where children are concerned, we should be careful and discriminating. We should take the time to thoroughly preview the television plans that the youngsters have and evaluate the effects of watching the programs on their developing minds. We should also monitor the amount of time a child spends watching television and make sure that it is time well spent; that is, time with educational or entertainment value for the viewer.

Be sure to hand in all revised drafts to your teacher for evaluation.

NOTES TO INSTRUCTOR

The following are suggestions and explanations about how to use *specific chapters* in the book. Please refer to these notes as you use each chapter.

INTRODUCTION

This section introduces students to the underlying philosophy on which the book is based. Read it aloud in class, either individually, or in groups. You could also assign groups a portion to read and ask them to report to the rest of the class about what they read. Because of the lengthy readings in this and all the other chapters, it is a good idea to stop every two or three paragraphs, and ask the students to summarize in the margin the key ideas. In this way, they are strengthening both reading skills and study skills.

We also recommend that instructors read portions and explain key points. In fact, it is always a good idea for you to read aloud a portion of the readings in the book to model correct pronunciation and intonation.

Though the texts have been chosen from newspapers and news articles from magazines in the United States, the topics are world-wide issues. As often as is appropriate, ask your students to share information from their native countries related to the topics.

EXERCISE 3: Revising the Draft, page xiv

Some students are not used to working in pairs or groups; this collaborative method is not always used in other countries. Explain that peer response is a valuable technique to learn so that they can use the feedback from a classmate in other classes as well, and for other tasks. It is an accepted way to learn in many classes here in the United States.

Have students read their revised drafts aloud to the class, or to their partner or group. Ask the listener to take notes about points that they liked or disliked in the draft.

Also have students write the introduction or another part of the draft on the board to get peer feedback. Model the correct kinds of feedback, not focusing just on grammar, but on ideas and the organization of the essay as well.

At this point students should understand the idea that peer feedback is one of the central focuses of the writing process pedagogy in this book. Remember, you can model peer response by making the class the group and acting as a group member yourself.

CHAPTER ONE

EXERCISE 4: Revising Questions, page 9

Revising questions should be answered by the students in writing groups or pairs. Model the answers to the Revising questions at first, until students get used to this kind of activity.

Try to help the students understand that revising (rethinking, reorganizing ideas for coherence, clarity, specificity, focus) is the step *before* editing for grammar and other English usage mistakes. The Writing Focus section of each chapter should help students understand ways to revise. Each Writing Focus is different in order to emphasize specific problems pertinent to learning to write argumentatively in English.

For both Revising and Editing, you may ask a student if copies could be made of his or her draft and distributed to the class for feedback. The Revising and Editing questions and Checklists can be used in groups with the copies of student drafts, also. They are simple questions to help focus and remind students of important issues and pitfalls that are common to most writers.

EXERCISE 6: The Editorial Board, page 13

Some students will find this exercise difficult, depending on how much they know about grammar, punctuation, and spelling in English. Try to use the students who are best at editing as editors, but most students at the advanced level can "hear" when something is wrong, even if they do not know the specific rule involved. Therefore, we recommend reading drafts aloud whenever possible.

Grammar is almost always an issue for all ESL students, even at the advanced level. What most of us do not realize is that while some more difficult rules have been acquired, like compounded tenses for example, often what is easier to teach and learn, like the subject-verb agreement rule, has not been acquired by the student, so that errors still surface in the writing. For this reason, we have given additional error analysis exercises in the chapters and in the Appendix so that students can practice recognizing, analyzing, and correcting errors, just as they must learn to do in their writing processes.

EXERCISE 10: Writing a Timed Essay, page 15

Time and topic writing is difficult for the timid writer. We suggest that you not grade the first composition that is done with the constraints of time, topic, and audience. Reassure students that practice will help alleviate anxiety and that they will have many more opportunities to practice in later chapters.

CHAPTER TWO

You may want to give the students some of the historical background of the shooting of Jim Brady and the origin of Sarah Brady's involvement with gun control.

EXERCISE 1: Cluster Diagram, page 18

The cluster diagram is just a means for mapping free-association. It is a simple focusing technique that compels students to plumb their imaginations for associations with a single concept. Write the central idea in the middle, then write ideas associated with it around the central idea. Unlike many types of diagrams, it is not ordered and linear. It can, however, help a writer locate ideas and make connections with a topic idea. We recommend modeling the cluster diagram on the board. Draw a circle with the word inside, then have the students call out associated words. Accept all suggestions, unless they are associations with new words; they should all be associations with the central word. Everyone's diagram might be unique. This technique really illustrates the creativity that is at the heart of composing.

Reading Selections, pages 19–24

Though the readings are about Hispanic students, bilingual education relates to other language populations as well. We recommend summarizing sections of the readings. Since the reading selections are lengthy, we suggest dividing them up in the following ways.

1. Read part of the selection aloud, taking turns.
2. Read part of the selection silently, taking notes.
3. Assign part of the selection as a take-home assignment.

It is important to distinguish between reading for content and reading literally. We recommend asking students to read the entire selection as fluently as possibly, only stopping occasionally to look up words in the Glossary. Ask them to think of it as a problem-solving activity, in which they have to discover or "guess" the main ideas, the main message in each passage. Explain the difference between reading holistically for meaning and reading literally in which each word is important.

CHAPTER THREE

Writing Focus: Improving Coherence, page 51

It is important to explain to students that linguistic research is suggesting that coherence in writing can vary from culture to culture, and it may be difficult for them to learn to write coherently in English at first. If your class needs more practice, bring in writing that has been published that is not particularly coherent, and pass out copies for class analysis.

Coherence is not an easy revision task, even for native speakers, so students will not be able to master it completely by the end of the chapter. The goal of this Writing Focus is to acquaint them with the issue so that they will be aware of coherence as a goal when they write and read their drafts.

CHAPTER FOUR

The Reading Selection in this chapter is long. You may want to divide it into sections and assign them for homework. The reason we used long selections in this book is to expose students to as much English written discourse as possible, and, of course, to give them a basis of concepts and vocabulary words with which to write their main composition assignment for each chapter.

EXERCISE 7: Doing Research, page 69

The exercise on doing research in this and other chapters may be presented as an assignment for extra credit for those students who are more fluent writers and have extra time.

CHAPTER FIVE

We realize that the abortion issue is a touchy subject for some people and some cultures. Therefore, we chose the scientific, balanced perspective evident in the writing of Sagan and Druyan. It is a challenge to guide the student away from emotionally biased points of view as the writers try to convince the reader of valid opinions worthy of the reader's consideration. Explain to the student that this chapter offers an opportunity for the student to get past emotional reaction so that all sides of the issues can be examined intellectually.

Writing the Draft, page 85

Because this is a complicated topic, you could brainstorm the options in the section Writing the Draft. You could even have a class debate, with a team assigned to each of the topics. After the debate/discussion, students may write their first draft, either as groups or individually.

EXERCISE 10: Verb Tense and Consistency, page 89

Students may find this difficult, so assign this based on your own discretion and intuition. It can also be used as an extra credit assignment. You will need to explain what is meant by the writer's "voice."

CHAPTER SIX

EXERCISE 1: Thinking About the Issue, page 94

After students have ranked the items in number 4, you can model the ranking of environmental hazard problems on the blackboard or pass out a sample. The object is to show how the average person's perceptions differ from those who are authorities on the topic of environmental ecology. You may have to explain the words for hazards that are not familiar to students.

Editing: Articles, page 105

If students have not progressed to the point where they can recognize and correct their English grammar and punctuation errors, you may want to have them complete the extra grammar exercises in the Appendices. You may also need to use a grammar book that emphasizes error analysis for second-language students. One we recommend is Patricia Byrd and Beverly Benson's *Improving the Grammar of Written English: The Handbook & The Editing Process* and accompanying handbook (Belmont, California: Wadsworth Publishing Company/Heinle & Heinle).

Many grammar items, like articles, are very complicated. You will not find a complete explanation in this book, rather a discussion of the key points.

We emphasize an error analysis approach because of our own research that discrete grammar exercises unrelated to actual communicative events are generally not as useful as teaching the uses and rules of a grammar item as they relate to the student's own writing. (See Watkins–Goffman and Berkowitz in *Research in the Teaching of Developmental Education*, October 1991). Help students become aware of which errors are developmental, or universal to developing writers, or related to structures in the native language and transferred to English inappropriately.

At this point, in Chapter Six, you might want to present a review of pertinent grammar rules. Then, for those who need extra help, assign the extra grammar exercises and error analysis practice that are in the Appendices.

CHAPTER SEVEN

This is the most challenging chapter of the book. You may need to model correct answers to exercises, explain, and generally lead the student through this chapter, particularly the Writing Focus.

Writing Focus: Analogy, page 117

Some students have difficulty with this way of writing argument. Explain that it is only one way of supporting an argument, and it is one of the possible ways of developing a writer's point of view. Indeed, there are times when analogy is more appropriate than other ways. Choose one successful student composition or the sample student draft on pages 118–119 and use it for a model for the class, so they can see an example of this technique of writing.

Additional Suggestions

Vocabulary

We suggest that you give a vocabulary "review activity" at this point so that students can reinforce vocabulary words learned. You can give a quiz, or ask for sentences using some words chosen from the vocabulary list in each chapter.

Writing Portfolio

Students can keep a folder, a writing portfolio in which they keep their drafts. As a review, have them look through their portfolios to find a draft that they would like to work through revision and editing processes. Or ask them to pick the draft they think is the best and the one they think is the worst. Tell them to check with the Revising questions to see if they can come up with reasons they chose the essays as examples. After completing the final chapter, students should hand in the writing portfolio to the instructor for evaluation of weaknesses and strengths developed through the course.

Evaluation of Drafts

There are many ways to evaluate student drafts. ESL students have a tendency to overemphasize grammar and editing concerns, which usually impedes proficient writing; therefore, we suggest the following:

1. Delay giving a grade until students have had practice writing drafts.
2. If possible, have individual conferences about the student's writing, giving positive as well as negative feedback. You can use the Revising questions included in each chapter as a guide.
3. Evaluate ideas first, giving specific comments or questions as feedback. Evaluate the mechanics second. If permissible, give two separate grades: one for content and one for form.

CHAPTER

▶ONE

Beyond the "Golden Door": The Homeless in Our Society

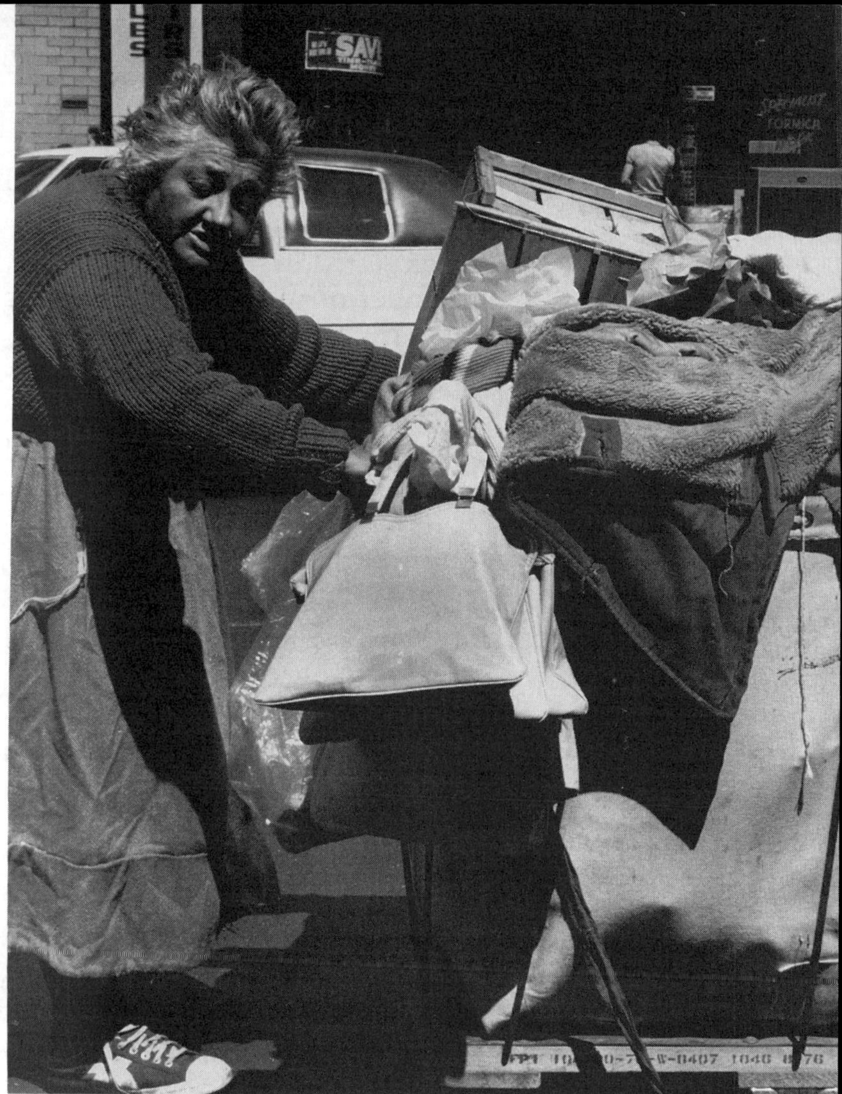

▶Prewriting

As discussed in the Introduction, prewriting is what you do in order to get started. In the following exercise, take notes as you discuss the answers to the questions on the topic. By taking notes, we mean simply that you should jot down any thoughts or ideas that occur to you during your group discussion. *Remember: when you take notes, you are writing the beginnings of a rough draft. Do* <u>*not*</u> *be concerned about spelling, punctuation, or grammar.* At this point you should only be concerned with generating ideas.

EXERCISE 1: Thinking About the Issue

In groups or pairs, discuss the answers to the following questions. Jot down ideas as you talk about this issue, and ask one member of the group to summarize the answers and share them with the rest of the class.

1. What would it be like to be homeless?
2. What exactly does the word "homeless" mean?
3. Cities are being overwhelmed by the problem of homelessness. Where have you seen homelessness? Describe what you saw.
4. In what ways has this problem affected you personally?
5. Why do you think we have so many homeless people in big cities? What do you think are the causes of homelessness?
6. Discuss this problem from the point of view of a homeless person, then from the point of view of the mayor of the city. How would the views of the residents of the city differ from those of people who have no place to live?
7. Ideally, what could government do to remedy the situation? Give at least one suggestion.

▶Reading Selection

In the following article from *The New York Times,* columnist Anna Quindlen discusses a way of coping with the problem of the homeless. After you have read it, write the answers to the discussion questions that follow.

Public & Private, Rooms of Their Own

by Anna Quindlen

1 When Ellen Baxter was working on a report about the homeless people of New York City, she went into **shelters** and subway stations and parks to talk to them about their lives. The problem was enormous but her conclusion was simple: "It was so obvious to me that what they wanted was a place to live," she says. "They wanted a key and a room where they could lock the door."

2 That was 10 years ago, and in that time the number of homeless people has multiplied and the patience of the public has worn thin. It seems the homeless have always been with us, and it's begun to occur to us that lots of them are people we don't like very much.

3 Ten years ago some of the homeless were older people, **disenfranchised** by misfortune or fire or expensive building rehabilitations. Some were former mental patients sent to the streets by government **policy** that said large institutions were an affront to humanity but provided few small ones in their place. "Lady, could you spare a quarter," said the men, their faces **vermillion** from years of Thunderbird. If a wild woman zoomed[1] by, shouting **imprecations** at President Kennedy and the Pope, you looked twice.

4 Today no one looks twice. The old homeless are still on the streets, but the holes in the societal safety net have **spit out** new companions. Young men **roving** the bus terminal, just out of jail, some of them, and seemingly looking for a way back in. Young women pushing strollers in midtown at midnight, tired of the four walls of the welfare hotel and three kids under the age of 4. In one subway station a homeless man lies on the floor at the foot of the stairs and orders **passersby**, "Put the money in the cup."

5 This has made people angry, and no wonder. Problem is, some of them get angry at the homeless. "Not in my neighborhood," we say about shelters, but it is already too late. If they're not in your neighborhood yet, sleeping in the doorways, looking through the **dumpsters** for dinner, they will be soon. To explain our antipathy[2] we say that the problem is too big and intractable[3] to solve.

6 While we've been saying that, people like Ellen Baxter have been quietly trying to solve it. In 1986, Ms Baxter opened The Heights in a stolid gray apartment building with a panoramic view of the feed[4] to the George Washington Bridge. The building is furnished with vanilla and gilt[5] French provincial furniture, a donation from the Pierre Hotel.

7 There are 55 permanent tenants, veterans of such diverse venues[6] as the 181st Street subway station, High Bridge Park and the Fort Washington Armory where 800 beds may be lined up

---

[1] zoom: speed or race noisily.
[2] antipathy: extreme dislike.
[3] intractable: difficult to manage.
[4] feed: highway entrance ramp.
[5] gilt: a thin layer of gold or gold-colored material applied to a surface.
[6] venue: location.

across the floor on any given night to welcome those who have no place to go. Visualizing it in the mind's eye makes it easy to understand why homeless people do not like shelters.

8 The people who live in The Heights, and the three other buildings Ms Baxter now **oversees**, are people with problems. They are people, some of them, who have smoked crack and passed out drunk and spent time in psychiatric wards, and who may do so in the future.

9 But they once were homeless and now are living with leases, with keys, some with jobs, all with dignity. Their subsidized rent comes out of a welter[7] of entitlement programs[8] and, in some cases, their own wages. They still may not be people we like very much. That shouldn't matter, but it does. We like to like the people we help, to have a poster child. It is time to grow up about this. Public policy cannot be determined by our collective warm fuzzies.

10 We may have one of two motives in this matter, vastly different but leading us to the same place. We can demand that government finance more small permanent residences like The Heights because that is the right thing to do, because we have looked into the faces of homeless men and women and occasionally recognized ourselves. That probably requires more than most of us can find within ourselves at this point, after explaining to our children why the man is swearing at the fire hydrant, after having someone urinate in our doorway.

11 So there is another reason to demand that government support those groups that have found humane and permanent solutions. The Heights costs about $15 per person per day, including the cost of its staff of social workers and counselors. The Armory, that vast expanse of temporary beds, costs at least twice that.

12 Look at it from a purely selfish point of view as well. You want the sidewalks and the parks to be clear again. You want to be left alone and not importuned[9] for a dollar a dozen times a day. And up in Washington Heights, and in other quietly compassionate

---

[7]welter: confused mass; jumble.
[8]entitlement program: a benefit program for public financial assistance.
[9]importuned: begged.

places all over this city, there are people who can help make that happen in a way that will not shame us as human beings.

Anna Quindlen, "Public & Private, Rooms of Their Own," *The New York Times*, 21 January, 1990.

EXERCISE 2: Understanding the Reading

Divide into groups or pairs. Write a brief answer (in complete sentences) to each of these questions. When you are finished, share your answers with the class. If you need to, refer back to the Quindlen article to find the needed information.

1. According to the author, what is the definition of a homeless person?
2. Why are some people angry at the homeless?
3. What does the author think should be done?
4. What other alternative solutions exist for the homeless?
5. What motives do people have to help the homeless?
6. Explain what is meant by "We have looked into the faces of homeless men and women and occasionally recognized ourselves." [par. 10]

EXERCISE 3: Vocabulary

1. The words listed below were highlighted in the text you just read. See if you can determine the meaning of each one from its context; then check the meaning listed in the glossary in the back of this book. (*Note:* Certain words or terms are used in particular ways that are not necessarily the most common. Be sure that you understand the definition of the word *as it is being used here,* not simply the most common dictionary definition. The glossary in the back of this book lists the meanings of words as they are used in each particular reading.)
2. Complete the sentences with an appropriate word from this vocabulary list (or a variation of it). In each case, the words are used in the same way (or one similar to that) as they were in the reading.

disenfranchised	passersby	shelters
dumpsters	policy	spit out
imprecations	roving	vermillion
oversees		

1. The dress she made and wore in the school play was such a bright ____________ that she stood out in the crowd scene.
2. Without money, property, or even the right to vote, the peasants in the small dictatorship felt totally ____________.
3. It is the ____________ of the city government to listen to the complaints of its citizens, and give them a reply.
4. Caroline went to the automated teller at the bank, inserted her card, punched some buttons, and much to her delight the thing ____________ $50 in cash.
5. Pickpockets ____________ throughout the crowd, spotting potential victims and making off with their wallets.
6. The garbagemen always empty all the cans on the block into the large ____________ behind the building.
7. The politician tried to speak to the angry crowd, but their loud ____________ drowned him out, so he left the stage.
8. Our apartment building was damaged by fire, and my sister had no room for us, so we had to stay in a ____________ for two weeks until we could move back home.
9. Now that she has been promoted to manager at the factory, Julia ____________ the work of eight other seamstresses.
10. When I was mugged, in broad daylight, in front of the supermarket, several ____________ came to my aid, chased the man, and got my pocketbook back for me.

▶Writing the Draft

TOPIC: The problem of homelessness is becoming more prevalent in the cities. What should be done to solve this problem?

Write an argument essay in which you state what you think should be done to resolve this problem, and defend your point of view.

1. To make sure you understand the topic, restate it in your own words.
2. Now write a draft in which you express your opinion on the issue of homelessness.
3. As discussed in the Introduction, the first paragraph should let the reader know that you understand the topic and have thought about your response. State your stand on the topic; at the end of the introduction, there should be no doubt in the reader's mind about what will follow in the next paragraphs.
4. Then, write two, three, or more supporting paragraphs using evidence to develop your main idea stated in your first paragraph. Remember: you may use evidence from your own experience and observation of life, such as what you have seen and read. (If you are using information from something you read, you must identify the source.)
5. The final paragraph, the conclusion, should reflect on the contents of the essay so far. When the reader has finished it, he or she will know that it is the end of the composition.
6. When you are finished writing, form groups in which to share your compositions.
7. Take turns reading the compositions aloud and commenting on what you hear.
8. Use the feedback from your classmates and your teacher when you revise.

Student Draft

After you have written your draft, look at this student draft.

Homelessness

1 Homelessness is a big problem in the city. There are homeless living in the parks. They are living in the streets. I know of a certain situation that is especially bad. This condition of these people give a bad view of the city.

2 Nowadays, this kind of situation could be from different kinds of problems. Such as unemployment, drugs, scarcity of housing, and high rent. Or, like a recent article from *The New York Times* discusses, deinstitutionalization of the mentally ill can cause a group of people to become homeless.

3 For instance in New York near the City Hall, a lot of people are living in a park. They are hanging tents to protect themselves from rain and cold, day and night. Some of these people have jobs. Which for some reason they lost, and with them their apartments. They don't accept living in shelters, and don't receive any help because they have no established address. About a few months ago the police forced these people to move from the park because it made the place look ugly; it was dirty and smelly. I think the government should do something to these homeless to help them find places with low rent.

4 However, some of these people have money but they don't want to pay rent, and refuse to live in shelters. For example, this lady came from Cuba a long time ago. She had her own apartment. Because she lost it in a fire. That accident was seven years ago. She does not have a family. She always sleeps inside or near the Lincoln Hospital. This lady is never clean and smells bad. When the administration of the hospital did a lot to help her. But she refused to receive any help. She does not want to live in a shelter, she said, "I prefer to sleep on the street."

5 The city government should give attention to the homeless. To make more houses with low rent. The city doesn't look nice. Also, the Mayor should order the homeless to have a check up because the entire city is infected with sick people.

6 My opinion is that this situation is due to neglect by the government. They should pay more attention to the problem. Make houses more comfortable for them and low rent. Homeless are all over the place. Are an embarrassment for all people. Visitors from other countries see these homeless sleeping on the streets. This gives a bad impression. The government should give more effort to this problem. This is the only way the city will change so it will look clean and beautiful like many years before. Tourists will want to come and visit again. The money they spend will help reimburse the government.

▶WRITING FOCUS: Using Personal Experience in Your Writing

Whether you agree or disagree with the opinions expressed by the author of this student draft, you probably recognize that it has certain strengths. One of the things this writer did effectively was to use a concrete example from her own experience to illustrate her point. By describing "this lady from Cuba" [par. 4], the writer compels the reader to visualize a real person, perhaps like someone the reader may already know.

Using personal experience in your writing is very valuable: it keeps you on solid ground, because you're writing about something you know; it forces you to use a narrative voice; it gets your reader involved. By carefully choosing appropriate, relevant personal experiences of your own to illustrate your opinions, you can add authority to your voice in argument writing.

There are other ways to improve drafts; some of these will be discussed in the *Revising* section.

▶Revising

EXERCISE 4: Revising Questions

Divide into groups. One person in each group will read the sample student draft to his or her group. The following questions will help you rethink the composition for organization, coherence (the smooth interconnection of ideas), and development of supporting points. When you have finished applying these questions to the sample essay, use them on your own draft.

1. Is the writer's main idea (his or her "point") stated clearly in the first paragraph? What is it?
2. Does each idea and each paragraph follow logically from one to the next? How does each idea *relate* to the one that precedes and follows it?
3. Are all ideas related specifically to the opinion being put forth in this draft? If not, which ones could be eliminated?
4. Which sentences explain, illustrate, or give examples about the topic?
5. What is the main idea of each paragraph? Is the idea adequately explained and developed?

6. Which ideas are particularly interesting? Could the writer add more details to develop this part of the draft? Could the writer have used details from *The New York Times* article about Ellen Baxter's solution for the homeless? Where should these details be included? (Remember: Whenever you use information from any source, you must attribute the information to that source. Whether you are making an exact quotation or just paraphrasing, you must tell the name of the author and the name and date of the publication where you found the information.)
7. Could a personal anecdote be added to make the argument more convincing? (Use the question words, *Who? What? Where? When? Why? How?* to help you develop your example with specific words.)
8. Does the conclusion seem to provide an adequate ending to the discussion of the topic?
9. Can you think of any questions that you could ask the writer that would help in the revision process?
10. Read the draft backwards (from the last paragraph to the first). Do you still feel that each paragraph is connected to the one preceding it?

Revised Student Draft

Below is a revised version of the student draft. In what ways is it better than the first draft?

Homelessness

1 Homelessness is a big problem in the city. There are homeless living in the parks and they are living in the streets. I know of a certain situation that is especially bad and give a bad view of the city.

2 Nowadays, this kind of situation could be from different kinds of problems, such as unemployment, drugs, scarcity of housing, and high rent. Or like a recent article from *The New York Times* suggests, deinstitutionalization of the mentally ill can cause a person to end up on the streets.

3 Some homeless have more hope and potential to improve their situation than others. For instance, in New York near the City Hall, a lot of people are living in a park. They are hanging tents to protect themselves from rain and cold, day and night. Some of

these people had jobs, which they lost for some reason, and with them, their apartments.

4 They could go to live in the subsidized housing of Ellen Baxter, if they could afford the extremely low rent. But some people refuse to live in shelters, and they can not receive help because they have no established address. What will happen to people like these?

5 A few months ago, the police forced these people to move from the park because they made the place look ugly. They were dirty and smelly. I think these people have lost all hope; they will never find better conditions. For example, there is a lady from Cuba who lost her apartment in a fire seven years ago. She does not have family. She sleeps near or inside Lincoln Hospital. The hospital administration offered to help her, but she refused their help. She said that she prefers sleeping on the street.

6 The city government should offer a solution to the situation of the homeless, including people like the lady from Cuba. People like her are an embarrassment, and should be told to get off the streets or they will go to jail. Then, when visitors come to our city, they will not leave with a bad impression. In addition, any money the city spent on shelters could be funded by profits from increased tourism. Most importantly, we, the decent citizens, could have our nice city back the way it was before homelessness became such a huge problem.

▶ SCREENING ROOM

You may wish to rent a video of the 1987 film *Ironweed.* Based on the Pulitzer Prize-winning novel of the same name by William Kennedy (who then adapted it into this screenplay), *Ironweed* features sensitive performances by Jack Nicholson and Meryl Streep in the roles of homeless persons struggling to survive in Albany, New York, in 1938.

EXERCISE 5: Thinking About the Movie

1. Write a summary of the events depicted in *Ironweed.*
2. Decide which character in the film was the most believable. Explain why you selected this character.

▶Editing: Sentence Structure

Many English-as-a-Second-Language students often make mistakes when writing English sentences even though they are placed in advanced classes. These errors are often noticeable as missing sentence parts, like a missing subject or verb, or incorrect punctuation; the results are most often seen as sentence fragments or run-on sentences.

There are eight basic sentence types in English.

1. The homeless man | coughed.
[subject | intransitive verb*]

2. The beggar | bothered | the businessman.
[subject | verb | object]

3. The poor woman | gave | her child | some bread.
[subject | verb | object 1 | object 2]

4. A homeless person | is | a human being.
[subject | BE verb | noun]

5. A drug addict | is | miserable.
[subject | BE verb | adjective]

6. The drug | seems | the solution.
[subject | linking verb | noun]

7. The soup | from the shelter | smells | delicious.
[subject | | linking verb | adjective]

8. The church | named | her | leader | of the homeless.
[subject | verb | object 1 | object 1a]

[The objects here were named 1 and 1a because they refer to the same idea. The objects in sentence number 3 refer to different ideas, so they are called object 1 and object 2.]

You will notice that while the sentences above differ in many ways, they all have a subject and verb. *Every English sentence must have both a subject and a verb;* it must begin with a capital

---

*Intransitive verb = verb that does not require an object

letter; it must end with a period, question mark, or exclamation point; and it must make sense, as a complete thought, even if you read it alone without the sentences before and after it. The sentences above are basic "kernel" sentences. They may have additional adjectives, adverbs, or prepositional phrases (like "from the shelter" in sentence 7). They may also have a *compound* (or multiple) subject or a compound verb.

Examples:

1. The homeless <u>mother and child</u> sought help in the shelter.
2. The volunteer <u>cooked</u> food and <u>provided</u> a bed.

EXERCISE 6: The Editorial Board

If you were an author who was going to publish a book, you would submit your writing to an editor or editors. Form an "Editorial Board" in each group and have the individuals in it (those who are particularly good at applying grammar, punctuation, and spelling rules) read your revised draft for errors. Each person should get a turn, including the "editors" themselves.

EXERCISE 7: Practice with Basic Sentence Patterns

The sentences below represent eight basic sentence patterns found in English. In the following sentences, find the subjects, verbs, objects, and adjectives. Then compare these sentences with the fragments in the next exercise.

1. The homeless are sad.
2. The government gives housing to the homeless.
3. We gave money.
4. The homeless often smell bad.
5. Billie Boggs was called a representative of the homeless.
6. Displaced people are often children.
7. The poor man coughed.
8. Later they called him a hero.

EXERCISE 8: Complete Sentences vs. Fragments

Read the following paragraphs, which contain both complete sentences and sentence fragments. Identify the fragments.

Then rewrite the paragraphs, fixing the fragments either by adding the missing parts or by combining fragments into complete sentences.

The terrible homelessness situation in this city. Some with jobs and some without. One man who was unemployed for over two years. Got a job with the Parks Department. He jumped for joy.

1991, a year of great hardship for middle class and poor people. Is hard to believe our leaders don't care. Ignoring all the most serious problems. Taxes are high. Businesses in danger of going under. Changes must come soon if disaster is to be avoided in our cities.

EXERCISE 9: Error Analysis

1. Look at the student draft on page 10 to find sentence structure and punctuation problems. Correct the mistakes and try to categorize them.
2. Look at your own revised draft(s); try to determine if there are punctuation errors, particularly sentence fragments or two sentences connected with commas. Make necessary corrections.
3. Identify and correct any other grammar errors.
4. What (if any) errors made by the writer of the student draft also occurred in your own draft?

Refer to Appendix page 136 for additional punctuation rules and exercises.

After you have received your classmates' feedback, revise and edit with the help of the preceding exercises. Then hand in the finished paper to your teacher for evaluation.

▶Writing with Time, Topic, and Audience Constraints

As college writers, you are often required to produce writing within specific constraints. Typically you are given a specific topic and a time limit. Another more subtle constraint is that of audience; that is, you must bear in mind exactly who will be reading what you write. For example, you would express yourself differently if you were writing two pieces about homelessness, one a letter to the editor of your local newspaper, the other a letter to a friend.

EXERCISE 10: Writing a Timed Essay

Within one hour, write a draft of an argument essay on one of the following three topics. Decide what your opinion is on the issue, and then argue for it.

1. Should handicapped people be the taxpayers' responsibility?
2. Should handicapped people (including the insane) be given special privileges in a democratic society?
3. Homeless children are becoming more numerous in the United States. Should tax moneys marked for defense be used instead to care for homeless children?

EXERCISE 11: Checklist for Time and Topic Writing

1. Were you able to complete the draft in one hour? Why or why not?
2. Divide into three groups. Group 1 should be in charge of sharing the theses that were developed on the preceding topics. Group 2 can share supporting paragraphs, and Group 3 can share the conclusions. How many points of view were there, and how many ways of supporting the topic? How do conclusions differ from group to group?

3. Remember: a personal anecdote can help develop ideas quickly. One reason for this is that you have more vocabulary words at your disposal when you are using the narrative mode, because it is more concrete and less abstract. Develop the main ideas in your example by answering the questions, *Who? What? Where? When? How? Why?* Then revise, including these answers in your draft wherever appropriate.

After you have received your classmates' feedback, revise and edit with the help of the preceding exercises. Refer to the Appendix for punctuation rules and exercises. Then hand in the paper to your instructor for evaluation.

CHAPTER ▸T W O

Gun Control vs. the Right to Bear Arms

▸Prewriting

In one memorable scene in the popular film *Raiders of the Lost Ark*, the hero Indiana Jones is confronted by a particularly fierce adversary. Jones' time appears to be up as his frighteningly powerful-looking foe brandishes an ancient weapon, a huge scimitar,[1] whirling it expertly about in preparation of killing Jones with it. The audience holds its breath... and then breathes a sigh of relief and a burst of laughter as Indy impatiently removes a pistol from his pocket and dispatches the threat with a pull of the trigger.

That brief scene worked so well and was so popular that it was reprised in the film's sequel. Why did it affect so many people so positively? Was it the contrast between an ancient and a modern

[1]scimitar: a large, curved sword.

weapon? Was it the difference between how one of us might feel and how Indiana Jones reacted? Was it simply the surprise when he solved the problem so easily?

One thing is for certain. The sight of that gun in the hand of that hero was a happy relief for millions of viewers concerned about their hero's well-being. But more often, particularly in light of recent waves of urban violence, the image of a gun does not provoke a happy response. More often it elicits terror and an image of the needless bloodshed of innocent people. In this chapter we will examine the issue of gun control and its implications in a democratic society.

EXERCISE 1: Cluster Diagram

Some objects call up many associations in people's minds. Divide into groups and try the following exercise, called a cluster diagram, to see what you associate with the word "gun."

1. Draw a circle one or two inches in diameter on a blank piece of paper, and write the word GUN inside it.
2. Stare at the word in the circle for a moment or two, and then draw an arrow from the circle outward, and write the first associated word that comes to your mind at the end of the arrow.
3. Now return your attention to the original word, GUN; then draw another arrow from the circle, in another direction, and write the next word that occurs to you while thinking about the original word.
4. Keep doing this until there is a large number of arrows and words emanating from the circle. (Don't ask yourself, "What word should I write next?" Try to let it flow automatically, almost without thought.)
5. You may not know why a certain word occurs to you until after you've written it and gone back and examined it later.
6. Try to always have the association be prompted by the original word, not by one of the associated words.

After you have finished with your cluster diagram, look it over and see if you understand *why* you wrote each word you did. Then compare the papers in your class or writing group. Are there some words that appeared on almost every cluster diagram? What about the ones that were unique to certain individuals—do those words indicate unique experiences associated with a gun?

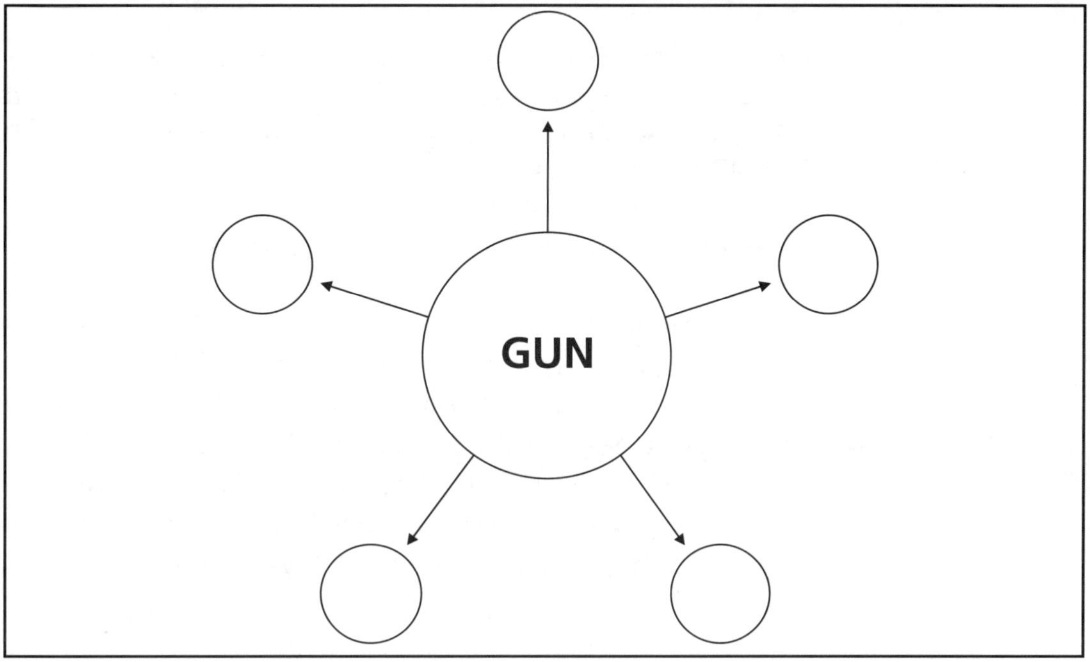

You may find that the word gun has very different meanings for different people. (Indeed, this is true for many words.)

▶Reading Selections

Following are two opinion essays that present opposing viewpoints about gun ownership and laws relating to gun ownership. They appeared side by side in *Time* on January 29, 1990. One of the authors is the executive vice-president of the National Rifle Association (NRA); the other is the leader of an organization called Handgun Control. Both of these organizations have a great many members who contribute money and time, much of which is used to attempt to convince lawmakers to behave in certain ways and enact specific laws regarding the ownership of guns.

As an aware adult, it is likely that you have opinions, possibly strong ones, leaning toward one and away from another of these arguments. Nevertheless, try to read both of them with as open a mind as possible. As you are reading, ask yourself these questions about the ideas being presented:

Are they truthful? Are they accurate? Does the writer have any hidden reasons for saying what he or she says? What are the important facts about guns? Is it easy to distinguish between facts and emotions?

The Case For Firearms...

The N.R.A.'s executive vice-president says guns will keep America free

by J. Warren Cassidy

1 The American people have a right "to keep and bear arms." This right is protected by the Second Amendment to the Constitution, just as the right to publish editorial comment in this magazine is protected by the First Amendment. Americans remain committed to the constitutional right to free speech even when their most powerful **oracles** have, at times, abused the First Amendment's **inherent** powers. Obviously the American people believe no democracy can survive without a free voice.

2 In the same light, the authors of the Bill of Rights knew that a democratic republic has a right—indeed, a need—to keep and bear arms. Millions of American citizens just as **adamantly** believe the Second Amendment is **crucial** to the maintenance of the democratic process. Many express this belief through membership in the National Rifle Association of America.

3 Our cause is neither trendy[1] nor fashionable, but a basic American belief that **spans** generations. The N.R.A.'s strength has never originated in Washington but instead has reached outward and upward from Biloxi, Albuquerque, Concord, Tampa, Topeka—from every point on the compass and from communities large and small. Those who fail to grasp this widespread commitment will never understand the depth of political and philosophical dedication symbolized by the letters N.R.A.

4 Scholars who have devoted careers to the study of the Second Amendment agree in principle that the right to keep and bear arms is **fundamental** to our concept of democracy. No high-court decision has yet found grounds to challenge this basic freedom. Yet some who oppose this freedom want to **waive** the constitutionality

[1]trendy: current; popular; fashionable.

of the "gun control" question for the sake of their particular—and sometimes peculiar—brand of social reform.

5 In doing so they seem ready, even eager, to disregard a constitutional right exercised by at least 70 million Americans who own **firearms**. Contrary to current antigun evangelism,[2] these gun owners are not bad people. They are hardworking, law abiding, tax paying. They are safe, sane, and courteous in their use of guns. They have never been, nor will they ever be, a threat to law and order.

6 History repeatedly warns us that human character cannot be scrubbed free of its defects through vain attempts to regulate **inanimate** objects such as guns. What has worked in the past, and what we see working now, are tough, N.R.A.-supported measures that punish the incorrigible[3] minority who place themselves outside the law.

7 As a result of such measures, violent crimes with firearms, like assault and robbery, have **stabilized** or are actually declining. We see proof that levels of firearm ownership cannot be associated with levels of criminal violence, except for their **deterrent** value. On the other hand, tough laws designed to **incarcerate** violent offenders offer something gun control cannot: swift, sure justice meted out[4] with no accompanying **erosion** of individual liberty.

8 Violent crime continues to rise in cities like New York and Washington even after severe firearm-control statutes[5] were rushed into place. Criminals, understandably, have illegal ways of obtaining guns. Antigun laws—the waiting periods, background checks, handgun bans, et al.—only **harass** those who obey them. Why should an honest citizen be deprived of a firearm for sport or self-defense when, for a gangster,[6] obtaining a gun is just a matter of showing up on the right street corner with enough money?

9 Antigun opinion **steadfastly** ignores these realities known to rank-and-file[7] police officers—men and women who face crime

[2]evangelism: the preaching and spreading of the word of the Gospel; or (as used here) the preaching and spreading of any strongly held idea or belief.

[3]incorrigible: incapable of being corrected or reformed.

[4]mete out: to deal out; to allot, as in portions.

[5]statute: law.

[6]gangster: criminal; particularly, a member of an organized gang; a racketeer.

[7]rank-and-file: the ordinary members of a group or organization, as opposed to its officers or leaders.

firsthand, not police administrators who face mayors and editors. These law enforcement professionals tell us that expecting firearm restrictions to act as crime-prevention measures is wishful thinking. They point out that proposed gun laws would not have stopped **heinous** crimes committed by the likes of John Hinckley Jr., Patrick Purdy, Laurie Dann, or mentally disturbed, usually addicted killers. How can such crimes be used as examples of what gun control could prevent?

10 There are better ways to advance our society than to excuse criminal behavior. The N.R.A. **initiated** the first hunter-safety program, which has trained millions of young hunters. We are the shooting sports' leading safety organization, with more than 26,000 certified instructors training 750,000 students and **trainees** last year alone. Through 1989 there were 9,818 N.R.A.-certified law-enforcement instructors teaching **marksmanship** to thousands of police officers.

11 Frankly, we would rather keep investing N.R.A. resources in such worthwhile efforts instead of spending our time and members' money **debunking** the failed and flawed promises of gun **prohibitionists**.

12 If you agree, I invite you to join the N.R.A.

J. Warren Cassidy, "The Case For Firearms...," *Time*, 29 January 1990, p. 22.

...And the Case Against Them

The head of Handgun Control says weapons are killing the future

by Sarah Brady

1 As America enters the next decade, it does so with an **appalling legacy** of gun violence. The 1980s were tragic years that saw nearly a quarter of a million Americans die from handguns—four times as many as were killed in the Vietnam War. We began the decade by witnessing yet another President, Ronald Reagan, become a victim of a would-be assassin's bullet. That day my husband Jim, his press secretary, also became a statistic in America's handgun war.

2 Gun violence is an **epidemic** in this country. In too many cities, the news each night reports another death by a gun. As dealers

push out in search of new addicts, Small-town, USA is introduced to the mindless gun violence **fostered** by the drug trade.

3 And we are killing our future. Every day a child in this country loses his or her life to a handgun. Hundreds more are permanently injured, often because a careless adult left within easy reach a loaded handgun purchased for self-defense.

4 Despite the **carnage**, America stands **poised** to face an even greater **escalation** of bloodshed. The growing popularity of military-style assault weapons could turn our streets into combat zones. Assault weapons, designed solely to mow down human beings, are turning up at an alarming rate in the hands of those most prone to violence—drug dealers, gang members, hate groups, and the mentally ill.

5 The Stockton, Calif., **massacre** of little children was a warning to our policymakers. But Congress lacked the courage to do anything. During the year of inaction on Capitol Hill, we have seen too many other tragedies brought about by assault weapons. In Louisville an ex-employee of a printing plant went on a shooting spree with a Chinese-made semiautomatic version of the AK-47, gunning down 21 people, killing eight and himself. Two Colorado women were murdered and several others injured by a junkie using a stolen MAC-11 semiautomatic pistol. And Congress votes itself a pay raise.

6 The National Rifle Association, meanwhile, breathes a sigh of relief, **gratified** that your attention is now elsewhere. The only cooling-off period the N.R.A. favors is a postponement of legislative action. It counts on public anger to fade before such **outrage** can be directed at legislators. The N.R.A. runs feel-good ads saying guns are not the problem and there is nothing we can do to prevent criminals from getting guns. In fact, it has said that guns in the wrong hands are the "price we pay for freedom." I guess I'm just not willing to hand the next John Hinckley a deadly handgun. Neither is the nation's law enforcement community, the men and women who put their lives on the line for the rest of us every day.

7 Two pieces of **federal legislation** can make a difference right now. First, we must require a national waiting period before the purchase of a handgun, to allow for a criminal records check.

Police know that waiting periods work. In the 20 years that New Jersey has required a background check, authorities have stopped more than 10,000 convicted **felons** from purchasing handguns.

8 We must also stop the sale and domestic production of semiautomatic assault weapons. These killing machines clearly have no legitimate sporting purpose, as President Bush recognized when he permanently banned their **importation**.

9 These public-safety measures are supported by the vast majority of Americans—including gun owners. In fact, these measures are so sensible that I never realized the campaign to pass them into law would be such an uphill battle. But it can be done.

10 Jim Brady knows the importance of a waiting period. He knows the living hell of a gunshot wound. Jim and I are not afraid to take on the N.R.A. leaders, and we will fight them everywhere we can. As Jim said in his congressional **testimony**, "I don't question the rights of responsible gun owners. That's not the issue. The issue is whether the John Hinckleys of the world should be able to walk into gun stores and purchase handguns instantly. Are you willing and ready to cast a vote for a common-sense public-safety bill **endorsed** by experts—law enforcement?"

11 Are we as a nation going to accept America's bloodshed, or are we ready to stand up and do what is right? When are we going to say "Enough"? We can change the direction in which America is headed. We can prevent the 1990s from being bloodier than the past ten years. If each of you picks up a pen and writes to your Senators and Representative tonight, you would be surprised at how quickly we could collect the votes we need to win the war for a safer America.

12 Let us enter a new decade committed to finding solutions to the problem of gun violence. Let your legislators know that voting with the gun lobby[1]—and against public safety—is no longer acceptable. Let us send a signal to lawmakers that we demand action, not excuses.

Sarah Brady, "...And the Case Against Them," *Time*, 29 January 1990, p. 23.

---

[1]lobby: a group of private individuals that works to have laws passed that will benefit its own special interests.

EXERCISE 2: Understanding the Readings

With other students, form a writing group, then write a one-sentence summary of each of the articles you just read. Both of your sentences should begin with the words "This writer believes...," and both of your sentences should have the word "because" somewhere in it.

Now that you have written down what each author believes and why he or she believes it, each group should read its summary sentences aloud. Then, discuss and answer the following questions.

1. Explain why one of the argument essays appealed to you more than the other. (Did one argument seem more intelligent, more rational, and less emotional than the other? Did one seem to offer clearer arguments than the other? Tell why.)
2. Explain why you *dis*agreed with any of the ideas presented.
3. Each writer seems to feel that the "vast majority of Americans" agree with his or her point of view, and that police officers in particular are on his or her side. Who is presenting the truth? Could they both be right? Why?
4. The writer from the N.R.A. mentions "the right to keep and bear arms," a reference to the Second Amendment to the U.S. Constitution. The writer in favor of tighter gun control asks support for "common-sense public-safety" laws that would restrict the individual's right to purchase and own guns. How do you feel about these points of view?
5. Both writers refer to John Hinckley, Jr. What link is there between Sarah Brady and Mr. Hinckley? What effect do you think this connection had on Mrs. Brady's feelings about gun control?
6. Now divide the class into two groups, one that favors the N.R.A.'s point of view, the other in favor of Handgun Control's position. (If necessary, form a third group of those who don't fully support either opinion.) Share your group's position with the rest of the class. Be sure to back up the position with specific evidence from the article, or your own experience.

EXERCISE 3: Vocabulary

adamantly	federal legislation	incarcerate	spans
appalling	felons	inherent	stabilized
carnage	firearms	initiated	steadfastly
crucial	fostered	legacy	testimony
debunking	fundamental	marksmanship	trainees
deterrent	gratified	massacre	trendy
endorsed	harass	oracles	waive
epidemic	heinous	outrage	
erosion	importation	poised	
escalation	inanimate	prohibitionists	

1. Write down, in your own words, a definition for each of the words highlighted in the reading selections. Use a dictionary to check your own accuracy. Since some words can have more than one meaning, make sure you're using the correct one for the context.
2. In the sentences below, nine words or phrases are highlighted. Each of these is an *antonym* (opposite) of one of the highlighted words in the texts you just read. Number a page 1–9, and write the word or phrase from the sentences below, and its antonym from the preceding readings.

1. The puppies were so **constantly active** in their kennel that it was difficult to count them.
2. Every person in my hometown is a **law-abiding citizen**.
3. The soldiers were thrilled that they could **liberate** the prisoners being held by the enemy.
4. By presenting all this evidence, I am **proving** my point.
5. These **experienced workers** have been on the job for over 12 years.
6. By wearing this button I **showed my opposition to** the candidate.
7. By increasing the number of police on the street, the town was able to realize a **decrease** in the intensity of its crime problem.
8. The firm was able to double its business when it set up a division for **overseas sales**.
9. The **incentive** for businesses to raise employee wages is the development of a stable, experienced workforce.

▶Writing the Draft

TOPIC: In an opinion essay of your own, tell how you feel regarding gun control: should the government pass more laws that would restrict the ownership, manufacture, and/or importation of guns? If yes, how far should the restrictions go? If no, how far should the freedom go? How is gun control handled in your native country?

1. Before writing, to make sure you understand the topic, restate it in your own words.
2. As discussed in the Introduction, the first paragraph should let the reader know what your position is and that you have thought about it.
3. Follow your opening with several supporting paragraphs that offer evidence to develop and reinforce your main idea stated in your first paragraph. Remember: you may use evidence from your own experience and observation of life, such as what you have seen and read. In addition, information found in the selections that you read in this chapter can be used as evidence to develop your argument. Your purpose—as always—is to convince your reader to agree with you.
4. The final paragraph should conclude your presentation and leave your reader ready to join you in whatever action you have suggested.

When you have finished your first or rough draft, set it aside for a time.

▶Revising

EXERCISE 4: Word Choice for Impact [Part 1]

Read the pairs of sentences that follow very carefully, especially the underlined words or phrases. In each pair, sentence A represents the word selection used by one of the essayists you read, and sentence B offers another word choice that means approximately the same thing. The author and paragraph number are indicated after each sentence so that you can go back and look at the context.

For each pair of sentences, explain in your own words why the writer chose A instead of B.

1. **A.** Assault weapons are designed solely to <u>mow down human beings</u>. [Brady, paragraph 4]
   B. Assault weapons are designed solely to <u>kill people rapidly</u>.
2. **A.** The Second Amendment is <u>crucial</u> to the maintenance of the democratic process. [Cassidy, paragraph 2]
   B. The Second Amendment is <u>important</u> to the maintenance of the democratic process.

3. **A.** The N.R.A. opposes the ideas of the gun prohibitionists. [Cassidy, paragraph 11]
   B. The N.R.A. opposes the ideas of the gun controllers.
4. **A.** America enters the next decade with an appalling legacy of gun violence. [Brady, paragraph 1]
   B. America enters the next decade with a history of gun violence.
5. **A.** Gun violence is an epidemic in this country. [Brady, paragraph 2]
   B. Gun violence is widespread in this country.

Student Draft

Here is a draft on gun control written by a student. As you read the writer's supporting paragraphs, ask yourself if she learned the lesson of Exercise 4, page 27.

Gun Control

1 The control of firearms has become more and more important in our society. Each day there are more accidents, murders, and abuse using firearms. The law does not help to control the use of guns.

2 In this country there is a law that says that anyone can have a gun. This law does not pay particular attention to what kind of people could have a gun or use it, in consequence there are lots of people who use guns and provoke a lot of problems.

3 I think that this law needs some changes to include some restrictions, because not everyone can have a gun. What I mean is that those people with mental health problems, those who have any connection with drugs or have enemies who they want to kill should not have a gun. When those people want to commit a crime they do not look around to see if any innocent bystanders are going to get hurt.

4 Every day there are more people who get hurt because of guns and drug users. I remember the case of that little girl who was killed while sleeping in her father's car that was a few months ago in Brooklyn. Some guys were fighting for something related to drugs and shooting at the place where the girl was. They had the right to live, now she is dead.

5 According to the Constitution of the United States, individuals

have the right to bear arms. The men in the example just mentioned do not have the right to use them to commit murder, they should be put in jail. All those who use guns should be able to understand how to use them and where.

6 In conclusion, I think that the law should be modified. It should say that everyone can have a gun if they need it. However, they should present proof of perfect mental health with no criminal record, or history of drug abuse.

▶WRITING FOCUS: Being Specific

When giving examples, stating ideas, asking questions, and making suggestions, it is always better to be more specific than general. Many student writers have a tendency to make broad, sweeping statements that are very general in nature; the more specific your comments are, the more able your reader is to understand exactly what you mean, and follow you as you try to make your point.

In the student essay you just read, there are a couple of instances of good use of specifics. In paragraph 4, she uses a specific example of a gun crime, telling the place, the time, and some detail. In the final sentence of the essay, she makes a moderately specific suggestion about criteria for the issuance of gun ownership permits. These things make the reader feel as though he is on solid ground, as opposed to the way he feels when he reads sentences such as the closing sentence of paragraph 5:

> All those who use guns should be able to understand how to use them and where.

By not backing up that sentence with some specificity, the writer leaves the reader wandering in a cloud of generality.

This Writing Focus is similar to the one in Chapter One, which reminds you that concrete examples from personal experience are good to use in an argument essay. Such examples naturally tend to be very specific. But even when you're discussing ideas, suggestions, etc., it is always a good idea to be as specific as you can.

EXERCISE 5: Evaluating the Draft

Answer the following questions as they relate to the student draft. When you finish, apply these same questions to your own rough draft.

1. How does the writer convince us (or fail to convince us) that she has had experience with and/or understanding of the problem of gun control?
2. Describe the organizational structure of the draft.
3. Could the writer have made the draft less repetitive? How? Could the writer have made the draft less confusing? How?
4. Give examples of specifics used by the writer in her explanations and development of her thesis.

EXERCISE 6: Seeing Both Sides

In constructing a convincing argument essay, it is always helpful to show that you understand the opposing point of view, and that you have good reasons for disagreeing with it. In this way you demonstrate your objectivity. You are saying, in effect, "I have looked carefully at both sides of this issue, considered the other point of view, and finally arrived at my point of view."

Divide into groups and do the following exercise. As group members, you are responsible for your own written answers, but you may assist each other in finding the correct answers.

1. Find instances in the Brady and Cassidy essays where the authors indicate an awareness of the opposing point of view.
2. How (if at all) does the author of the student draft above demonstrate an understanding of both sides of the issue?
3. Now examine your rough draft. Presumably, you have clearly stated your opinion about gun control. (Make sure you have done so.) Now ask yourself, "Does my essay show that I have arrived at my opinion after considering *both sides* of the issue? Could I make my essay more convincing by emphasizing this more?"

EXERCISE 7: Getting Personal

1. Find someone (not yourself) who has had a personal experience with a violent incident involving a gun—a police officer, a soldier, a crime victim, a criminal, a witness.

2. Question that person about his or her feelings regarding gun control. Then, revisit your own feelings as expressed in your essay.
3. Report back to the class on whether your feelings have changed or been confirmed.
4. How could this incident be used as evidence in a composition about gun control, pro or con?
5. Now, divide into groups. See what the consensus of opinion is in your group. Write a summary of your group's position.

EXERCISE 8: Revising Questions

Divide into groups. One person in each group will read each draft to his or her group. The following questions will help you rethink the composition for organization, coherence, and development of supporting points.

1. Is the writer's main idea (his or her "point") stated clearly in the first paragraph? What is it?
2. Does each idea and each paragraph follow logically from one to the next? How does each idea *relate* to the one that precedes and follows it?
3. Are all ideas related specifically to the opinion being put forth in this draft? If not, which ones could be eliminated?
4. Which sentences explain, illustrate, or give examples about the topic?
5. What is the main idea of each paragraph? Is the idea adequately explained and developed?
6. Which ideas are particularly interesting? Could the writer add more details to develop this part of the draft? (Could the writer have used information from one or the other of the articles from *Time* on the topic of gun control as evidence to support a point of view? Where should these details be included?)
7. Could a personal anecdote be added to make the argument more convincing? (Use the question words, *Who? What? Where? When? Why? How?* to help you develop your example with specific words.)
8. Does the conclusion seem to provide an adequate ending to the discussion of the topic?
9. Can you think of any questions that you could ask the writer that would help in the revision process?

10. Read the draft backwards (from the last paragraph to the first). Do you still feel that each paragraph is connected to the one preceding it?

Having carefully applied the concepts of Exercises 5–8 to your rough draft, now go back and actually revise your draft. Remember, you need not pay attention at this point to spelling, punctuation, capitalization, and other matters of form; the revising stage applies only to the selection and expression of ideas. Editing can be done later.

▶ SCREENING ROOM

A movie is available in video stores that depicts the life and struggles of James Brady, the husband of Sarah Brady. Brady was President Reagan's press secretary; he was critically wounded in the attempt on Reagan's life in 1981. Since that time, he and his wife have become leaders of the gun control movement. The 1990 film, featuring Beau Bridges in the title role, is called *Without Warning: The James Brady Story.*

EXERCISE 9: Thinking About the Movie

1. After you view the videotape, write a short summary of the events that took place in the movie.
2. List any new ideas you gained that could be used for support (on either side of the issue) in your composition on the topic of gun control.

▶Editing: Compound Sentences and Punctuation

In Chapter One we examined the simple sentence. Now we will take a look at compound sentences. These are two complete sentences joined by conjunctions such as *and, or,* or *but.* (Two complete sentences may also be joined by *for, yet* or *nor.*)

Examples:

1. The gun control legislation is on the front page of the news, *and* politicians are using the issue for a campaign platform.
2. Sarah Brady is coming from a personal experience, *but* not everyone has had Jim Brady's misfortune at the end of a gun.
3. You can believe in the right to bear arms, *or* you can try to defend the innocent victims from maniacs.

Notice that each of the three compound sentences contains a pair of simple sentences joined by a comma and a conjunction: *and, or,* or *but.* Never join the two parts of a compound sentence with a comma only.

EXERCISE 10: Compound Sentences

1. Look at the student draft on pages 28–29 and see if you can find an error with punctuation, in which two complete simple sentences are joined only by a comma.
2. Rewrite the sentences correctly, as a compound sentence with a comma and a conjunction.
3. Examine your own draft to be sure that the compound sentences, if included, are correctly formed.

Refer to the Appendix for additional punctuation rules and exercises. After you have received your classmates' feedback, revise and edit your draft with the help of the preceding exercises. Then hand in the finished copy to your instructor for evaluation.

OPTIONAL EXERCISE: Word Choice for Impact [Part 2]

In the first sentence of paragraph 3 of the Cassidy essay, he makes the very unusual statement "Our cause is neither trendy nor fashionable...." In the essay by Ms. Brady (last sentence of paragraph 5), there appears the seemingly irrelevant comment: "And Congress votes itself a pay raise."

Go back and reread these two passages in their original context. Do you understand what the authors were attempting to accomplish with these particular passages? Were they successful—that is, did they accomplish their aims when you read the essays the first time? Explain.

▶Writing with Time, Topic, and Audience Constraints

EXERCISE 11: Writing a Timed Essay

It has been argued that the U.S. criminal justice system is not fair, that many criminals who are truly dangerous to society go free, while other people are often accused and punished unfairly.

Some even say that racial prejudice is evident in sentencing, and that people who are minorities tend to get tougher verdicts.

Divide into small discussion groups. Poll each member of your group on the following questions:

1. Do you believe the charges (in the paragraph above) to have validity?
2. Cite at least one specific example which shows that the U.S. justice system is fair or unfair.
3. In your opinion, how does the American justice system compare with that of other countries with which you are familiar?

After considering the opinions offered and the examples cited by your fellow group members, write a draft on the topic "Fairness in the Criminal Justice System." Allow yourself no more than one hour (from prewriting to final copy).

CHAPTER ▶THREE

Bilingual Education: Help or Hindrance?

▶Prewriting

The educational system of the United States has been severely criticized by the public media over the last three decades. Inadequate curricula, over-crowded classrooms, low reading scores, and poor selection of teachers are but a few aspects of education that the American public uses to criticize our failing schools. This situation caused the Carnegie Foundation for the Advancement of Teaching to provide funds to conduct a three-year study to inquire about the status of public education in inner-city schools. Some of the findings of that study questioned the effectiveness of the bilingual mode of instruction for teaching children whose native language is other than English. Bilingual education is a method for working with students whose native language is not English. It offers these students content courses taught in their native language, and concurrently provides classes in English-as-a-Second-Language to assist those students in their acquisition of English.

As a student, how do you feel about American schooling, especially the education of immigrant, non-English-speaking students?

EXERCISE 1: Thinking About the Issue

Divide into pairs or groups and do the following:

1. Make a list of the good aspects of American schools.
2. Make another list of the aspects of U.S. public education that you feel need improvement.
3. Which of the characteristics you listed focuses on the plight of immigrant students in American schools?
4. If you are familiar with the educational system of a country other than the United States, compare the two systems. Be specific and give examples.
5. If you could, what would you change in the U.S. educational system for yourself? For your children?

After discussion in groups, come together and share your ideas with the entire class.

▶Reading Selections

Following are two opposing position papers written by two prestigious Hispanic Americans. Angelo Gonzalez is executive director of ASPIRA of New York, Inc., an Hispanic advocacy and civic organization. Richard Rodriguez is a well-known writer and educator. He is the author of *Hunger of Memory*, a first-person account of second language acquisition.

Bilingualism, Pro: The Key to Basic Skills, Native Language Held Vital to Self-Esteem and Motivation

by Angelo Gonzalez

1 If we accept that a child cannot learn unless taught through the language he speaks and understands; that a child who does not speak or understand English must fall behind when English is the dominant **medium** of instruction; that one needs to learn English so as to be able to participate in an English-speaking society; that self-esteem and motivation are necessary for effective learning; that rejection of a

child's native language and culture is **detrimental** to the learning process: then any necessary effective educational program for limited or no English-speaking ability must incorporate the following:

- Language arts and comprehensive reading programs taught in the child's native language.
- Curriculum content areas taught in the native language to further comprehension and academic achievement.
- Intensive instruction in English.
- Use of materials sensitive to and reflecting the culture of children within the program.

2 **Most Important Goal.** The **mastery** of basic reading skills is the most important goal in primary education since reading is the basis for much of all **subsequent** learning. Ordinarily, these skills are learned at home. But where beginning reading is taught in English, only the English-speaking child profits from these early acquired skills that are **prerequisites** to successful reading development. Reading programs taught in English to children with Spanish as a first language wastes their acquired linguistic attributes and also **impedes** learning by forcing them to absorb skills of reading simultaneouly with a new language. Both local and national research **data** provide **ample** evidence for the efficacy[1] of well-implemented programs. The New York City Board of Education Report on Bilingual Pupil Services for 1982–83 indicated that in all areas of the curriculum—English, Spanish, and mathematics—and at all grade levels, students demonstrated **statistically** significant gains in tests of reading in English and Spanish and in math. In all but two of the programs reviewed, the attendance rates of students in the program, ranging from 86 to 94 percent, were higher than those of the general school population. Similar higher attendance rates were found among students in high school bilingual programs.

3 At Yale University, Kenji Hakuta, a **linguist,** reported recently on a study of working-class Hispanic students in the New Haven bilingual program. He found that children who were the most bilingual, that is, who developed English without the loss of Spanish, were brighter in both verbal and nonverbal tests. Over time, there was an increasing **correlation** between English and

[1]efficacy: usefulness; worthiness.

Spanish—a finding that clearly contradicts the charge that teaching in the home language is detrimental to English. Rather the two languages are **interdependent** within the bilingual child, reinforcing each other.

4 **Essential Contribution.** As Jim Cummins of the Ontario Institute for Studies in Education has argued, the use and development of the native language makes an essential contribution to the development of minority children's subject-matter knowledge and academic learning potential.

5 In fact, at least three national databases[2]—the National **Assessment** of Educational Progress, National Center for Educational Statistics—High School and Beyond Studies, and the Survey of Income and Education—suggest that there are long-term positive effects among high school students who have participated in bilingual-education programs. These students are achieving higher scores on tests of verbal and mathematical skills.

6 These and similar findings buttress[3] the argument stated persuasively in the recent joint recommendation of the Academy for Educational Development and the Hazen Foundation, namely, that America needs to become a more multilingual nation and children who speak a non-English language are a national resource to be **nurtured** in school.

7 Unfortunately, the present Administration's educational policies would seem to be leading us in the opposite direction. Under the **guise** of protecting the common language of public life in the United States, William J. Bennett, the Secretary of Education, unleashed a frontal attack on bilingual education. In a major policy address, he engaged in **rhetorical** distortions about the nature and effectiveness of bilingual programs, pointing only to unnamed negative research findings to justify the Administration's **retrenchment** efforts.

8 Arguing for the need to give local school districts greater flexibility in determining appropriate methodologies in serving limited-English-**proficient** students, Mr. Bennett fails to realize that, in fact, districts serving large numbers of language minority students, as is the case in New York City, do have that flexibility. Left to their own devices in **implementing** legal mandates,[4] many school

---

[2]database: a large collection of information in a computer memory.

[3]buttress: give support to.

[4]mandate: a legal command or instruction.

districts have performed poorly at providing services to all **entitled** language-minority students.

9 **A Harsh Reality**. The harsh reality in New York City for language-minority students was documented comprehensively last month by the Educational Priorities Panel. The panel's findings revealed that of the 113,831 students identified as being limited in English proficiency, as many as 44,000 entitled students are not receiving any bilingual services. The issue at hand is, therefore, not one of choice but rather violation of the rights of almost 40 percent of language-minority children to equal educational opportunity.

10 In light of these findings the Reagan Administration's recent statements only serve to exacerbate[5] existing **inequities** in the American educational system for linguistic-minority children. Rather than adding fuel to a misguided debate, the Administration would serve these children best by insuring the full funding of the 1984 Bilingual Education Reauthorization Act as passed by the Congress.

Angelo Gonzales, "Bilingualism, Pro: The Key to Basic Skills, Native Language Held Vital to Self-Esteem and Motivation," *The New York Times*, 10 November, 1985.

---

[5]exacerbate: make worse; aggravate.

Bilingualism, Con: Outdated and Unrealistic
by Richard Rodriguez

1 How shall we teach the dark-eyed child *inglés*? The debate continues much as it did two decades ago.

2 Bilingual education belongs to the 1960s, the years of the black civil rights movement. Bilingual education became the official Hispanic demand; as a symbol, the English-only classroom was intended to be analogous[1] to the segregated lunch counter, the locked school door. Bilingual education was **endorsed** by judges and, of course, by politicians well before anyone knew the answer to the question: Does bilingual education work? Who knows? *¿Quién sabe?*

3 The official drone[2] over bilingual education is conducted by educationists with numbers and charts. Because bilingual education

---

[1]analogous: comparable.
[2]drone: a dull background noise.

was never simply a matter of pedagogy, it is too much to expect educators to resolve the matter. Proclamations concerning bilingual education are weighted at bottom with Hispanic political **grievances** and, too, with middle-class romanticism.

4 No one will say it in public; in private, Hispanics argue with me about bilingual education and every time it comes down to memory. Everyone remembers going to that grammar school where students were slapped for speaking Spanish. Childhood memory is offered as **parable**; the memory is meant to **compress** the gringo's long history of offenses against Spanish, Hispanic culture, Hispanics.

5 It is no coincidence that, although all of America's ethnic groups are implicated in the policy of bilingual education, Hispanics, particularly Mexican Americans, have been its chief **advocates.** The English words used by Hispanics in support of bilingual education are words such as "dignity," "heritage," "culture." Bilingualism becomes a way of exacting from gringos a grudging admission of **contrition**—for the 19th century theft of the Southwest, the relegation[3] of Spanish to a foreign tongue, the injustice of history. At the extreme, Hispanic bilingual enthusiasts demand that public schools "maintain" a student's sense of separateness.

6 Hispanics may be among the last groups of Americans who still believe in the 1960s. Bilingual education proposals still serve the romance of that decade, especially of the late '60s, when the heroic black civil rights movement grew **paradoxically** wedded to its opposite—the ethnic revival movement. Integration and separatism merged into twin, possible goals. With integration, the black movement inspired middle-class Americans to imitations—the Hispanic movement; the Gray Panthers; feminism; gay rights. Then there was withdrawal, with black glamour leading a romantic retreat from the anonymous crowd.

7 Americans came to want it both ways. They wanted in and they wanted out. Hispanics took to celebrating their diversity, joined other Americans in dancing rings around the melting pot.

8 **Mythic Metaphors**. More intently than most, Hispanics wanted the romance of their dual cultural allegiance backed up by law.

---

[3]relegate: to assign to a less important position.

Bilingualism became proof that one could have it both ways, could be a full member of public America and yet also separate, private, Hispanic. "Spanish" and "English" became mythic metaphors, like country and city, describing separate islands of private and public life.

9 Ballots, billboards, and, of course, classrooms in Spanish. For nearly two decades now, middle-class Hispanics have had it their way. They have foisted[4] a neat ideological **scheme** on working-class children. What they want to believe about themselves, they wait for the child to prove that it is possible to be two, that one can assume the public language (the public life) of America, even while remaining what one was, existentially separate.

10 Adulthood is not so neatly balanced. The tension between public and private life is **intrinsic** to adulthood, certainly middle-class adulthood. Usually the city wins because the city pays. We are mass people for more of the day than we are with our intimates. No Congressional mandate or Supreme Court decision can diminish the loss.

11 I was talking the other day to a carpenter from Riga, in the Soviet Republic of Latvia. He has been here six years. He told me of his having to force himself to **relinquish** the "luxury" of reading books in Russian or Latvian so he could begin to read books in English. And the books he was able to read in English were not of a complexity to satisfy him. But he was not going back to Riga.

12 Beyond any question of pedagogy there is the simple fact that a language gets learned as it gets used. One fills one's mouth, one's mind, with the new names for things.

13 The civil rights movement of the 1960s taught Americans to deal with forms of discrimination other than economic—racial, sexual. We forget class. We talk about bilingual education as an ethnic issue; we forget to notice that the program mainly touches the lives of working-class immigrant children. Foreign-language acquisition is one thing for the upper-class child in a convent school learning in French to curtsy.[5] Language acquisition can

---

[4]foist: to force upon another, as by trickery.

[5]curtsy: a gesture of respect or reverence, made by women by bending the knees with one foot forward.

only seem a loss for the ghetto child, for the new language is psychologically **awesome,** being, as it is, the language of the bus driver and papa's employer. The child's difficulty will turn out to be psychological more than linguistic because what he gives up are symbols of home.

14 **Pain and Guilt**. I was that child! I faced the stranger's English with pain and guilt and fear. Baptized to English in school, at first I felt myself drowning—the ugly sounds forced down my throat until slowly, slowly (held in the tender grip of my teachers), suddenly the conviction took hold: English was my language to use.

15 What I **yearn** for is some candor from those who speak about bilingual education. Which of its supporters dares speak of the price a child pays—the price of adulthood—to make the journey from a working-class home into a middle-class schoolroom? The real story, the silent story of the immigrant child's journey is one of embarrassments in public; **betrayal** of all that is private; silence at home; and at school the hand tentatively raised.

16 Bilingual enthusiasts bespeak[6] an easier world. They seek a linguistic solution to a social dilemma. They seem to want to believe that there is an easy way for the child to balance private and public, in order to believe that there is some easy way for themselves.

17 Ten years ago, I started writing about the ideological implications of bilingual education. Ten years from now some newspaper may well invite me to contribute another Sunday **supplement** essay on the subject. The debate is going to continue. The bilingual establishment is now inside the door. Jobs are **at stake**. Politicians can only count heads; growing numbers of Hispanics will insure the **compliance** of politicians.

18 Publicly, we will continue the fiction. We will solemnly address this issue as an educational question, a matter of pedagogy. But privately, Hispanics will still seek from bilingual education an admission from the gringo that Spanish has value and presence. Hispanics of middle class will continue to seek the romantic assurance of separateness. Experts will argue. Dark-eyed children will sit in the classroom. Mute.

[6]bespeak: foretell.

Richard Rodriguez, "Bilingualism, Con: Outdated and Unrealistic," *The New York Times,* 10 November, 1985.

EXERCISE 2: Understanding the Readings

Divide into groups and do the following.

1. Summarize the point of view of each writer.
   a. Carefully reread each article.
   b. In your own words, restate what you just read.
   c. Be careful to stick only to what you read, NOT your opinion.
   d. Read your summary over; then compare yours with that of a classmate. Make sure no central points have been omitted.
2. What evidence does the first writer use to support his thesis?
3. What evidence does the second writer use to make his point?
4. Identify any passages in which either writer addresses the opposing point of view.
5. Which writer is more convincing? Why? Indicate specific passages in the reading that helped you decide.
6. Describe your position on the issue of bilingual education. What evidence would you use to support your position?

EXERCISE 3: Defining New Words

Define the words given below after trying to determine their meaning from the context. Check your guess with the Glossary in the back of this text. After you have learned the exact meanings of these words, reread the selection to further your understanding of the new vocabulary.

Bilingual Education: Pro

ample	guise	mastery	retrenchment
assessment	impede	medium	rhetorical
correlation	implement	nurture	statistical
data	inequities	prerequisites	subsequent
detrimental	interdependent	proficient	
entitled	linguist		

Bilingual Education: Con

advocate	compress	metaphor	relinquish
assurance	contrition	mute	retreat
at stake	endorsed	mythic	scheme
awesome	grievance	parable	supplement
betrayal	intrinsic	paradox	yearn
compliance	merge		

EXERCISE 4: Vocabulary

Complete the sentences in the following draft with words (or formations of words) from the vocabulary lists just given.

Before Louise moved to Canada, she went to the library to assemble as much ______________ [noun] information about the country as she could. She learned that her inability to speak French would ______________ [verb] hold back, slow her ability to communicate in some areas. She thought the problem was ______________ [adjective] very large, because it would take a long time before she could become ______________ [adjective] competent; able to use something in that language. Eventually, since her entire future and the future of her family was ______________ [adjective phrase] dependent upon; at risk, she came up with a clever ______________ [noun] a plan. She would get a job in which French was not a ______________ [noun] a prior requirement; something one needs in order to begin; through the ______________ [noun] a means of communication of French television and movies, she would immerse herself in the language. She was not a ______________ [noun] expert in language studies; one who speaks several languages fluently but she was sure that in this way she would soon develop a ______________ [noun] proficiency; competence; ability to control something of the new language. Because she ______________ [verb (with *-ed* added to vocabulary word)] desire; want so to learn it, she was able to ______________ [verb] squeeze together; confine to a smaller than usual area months of learning into a few weeks. Most importantly, she did not need to remain ______________ [adjective] unable to speak when someone spoke to her in French.

EXERCISE 5: Researching a Topic

You may do the following as a group or on your own:

1. In the periodical section of your library identify two or three newspaper or magazine articles on bilingual education. (Include authors who have different points of view.) Read them carefully.
2. Summarize the articles you read.
3. Be sure to write the author's name, the name of the publication in which it appeared, the date, the section, and the page number.
4. On another sheet of paper or card, write your opinion of the articles you just summarized.
5. Share what you learned with your writing group or partner.
6. Did any information you gained doing this exercise change your opinion on the topic? If you have formed groups, please share your insights with the group; if you did the exercises individually, share your insights with the class.

Using Other Sources

Your argument essays are always strengthened when you use information obtained from authoritative sources. If you find a statistic that pertains to your thesis, it can certainly make your argument stronger. If you discover a statement from some individual who is in a position to really know firsthand about an issue, you should include that statement if it furthers your purpose. If you learn something that advances your understanding of a topic, share it with your reader. All of these things ought to be included to make your argument stronger. It is vital, however, to let your reader know the original source of ideas which are not originally your own.

Using information from a source other than yourself, either by copying it or paraphrasing it, without telling the reader who the source is, is called *plagiarism.* Whether it is accidental or intentional, it is stealing someone else's work, and it is illegal.

To avoid plagiarism is simple: always give credit for information that comes from someone else's ideas. That is, cite the source from which the information came. This is usually done with a footnote of one sort or another. Footnotes can appear at the end of a sentence, at the end of a paragraph, at the bottom ("foot") of a page, or at the end of a paper.

Exactly what should be footnoted and what should not? Generally speaking, any information you gathered in the process of researching your essay or report should be footnoted. An exception is information that is common knowledge, or that is readily available from a variety of sources. For example, you may have learned the fact that Jupiter is the fifth planet from the sun while researching a report, but since that information could be found in any book on the subject, it is not absolutely necessary to footnote it. However, if you included more specific information, about Jupiter's 16 moons, its magnetic field, or its chemical makeup, this information should be given a footnote so that your reader knows where you obtained it.

Of course, if you use someone else's words exactly as they were written or spoken, this must always be footnoted. It should also be surrounded by quotation marks (" ") to show that it is an exact quotation.

If information is in any way controversial, or subject to disagreement, it is always best to footnote it. For example, you would not need to provide a footnote if you mentioned the fact that Babe Ruth hit 60 home runs for the New York Yankees in 1927. However, if you wrote that "Ruth is considered the greatest all-around player who ever lived," there are those who might disagree, so it is best that you cite at least one authoritative source to back up your claim.

Footnotes, therefore, serve several purposes. They enable you to "borrow" information from a variety of sources and use it in a fair and open manner. They also tell your reader that you have done research, and that your information is not made up, but rather comes from a reliable source.

If you are unsure whether or not to footnote something, footnote it. You can be wrong for not doing it, but you can't be wrong by doing it.

The most efficient way to mark a footnote is to place the identifying footnote number at the end of the sentence that contains information you learned from one of your sources. In the footnote citation, place the last name of the author of the work cited, followed by a comma and the page number on which the cited material appears. The reader interested in following up on the material can then find it in your bibliography.

Example A: To paraphrase material (with a citation):

The basic noun/verb distinction is universally found in human language, but is expressed more differently from one language to another than might be anticipated. An element may be a noun in one language or a verb in another, or vice versa (Elgin, 8).

Example B: If the author being cited is mentioned in your sentence, you should simply refer to the page number of the text:

Linguist Elgin says that the basic noun/verb distinction is universally found in human language, but is expressed more differently from one language to another than might be anticipated. An element may be a noun in one language or a verb in another, or vice versa (8).

If you use a direct quotation, be sure you have a reason for using it, and that it fits in the context of what you are trying to communicate. Be sure to use quotation marks (" ") around the material you are quoting verbatim. Then, include a citation as in Example A. These citations refer your reader to the bibliography. In the bibliography, list a complete description of the material you have cited in your paper. The reader will see that one of the books or articles you cited is by Dr. Suzette Haden Elgin, and your bibliographic entry will include enough information to identify the source completely. A bibliography entry for a book would look like this:

Elgin, Suzette H. *What is Linguistics?* Englewood, N.J. Prentice Hall, Inc. 1979.

For a magazine article:

Klima, Ethan. "Relatedness Between Grammatical Structures." *Language,* 1964:40.

For a newspaper article:

Wilford, John Noble, "What Doomed the Maya? Maybe Warfare Run Amok." *The New York Times,* 19 November, 1991: C1, 6-7.

The preceding examples conform to the *Modern Language Association* (MLA) *Style Manual.* Ask your instructor which style is preferred in your class.

▶Writing the Draft

TOPIC: "Bilingual Education is an effective way to educate people whose native language is not English." Do you agree or disagree? Give reasons why and be specific.

Remember:

1. Write an introduction stating your main idea. You may include some supporting ideas that can be developed later.
2. Write the body of the composition. Include at least two paragraphs giving illustrations, anecdotes, or factual evidence. You may also use a comparison to explain your perspective. If you have facts on hand about the topic, you may use these supporting ideas in order to make your point. (See the preceding exercise.)
3. The conclusion should summarize the position you have just discussed. It can also ask questions about, reflect upon, or analyze the topic.

▶Revising

EXERCISE 6: Revising Questions

Divide into groups or pairs, exchange papers, and apply these questions to the new draft.

1. Is the writer's main idea (his or her "point") stated clearly in the first paragraph? What is it?
2. Does each idea and each paragraph follow logically from one to the next? How does each idea *relate* to the one that precedes and follows it?
3. Are all ideas related specifically to the opinion being put forth in this draft? If not, which ones could be eliminated?
4. Which sentences explain, illustrate, or give examples about the topic?
5. What is the main idea of each paragraph? Is the idea adequately explained and developed?
6. Which ideas are particularly interesting? Could you add more details to develop this part of the draft? (Could you have used details from *The New York Times* articles about bilingual education? Where should these details be included? Did you document the source to avoid plagiarism?)
7. Could a personal anecdote be added to make the argument more convincing? (Use the question words, *Who? What? Where? When? Why? How?* to help you develop your example with specific words.)

8. Does the conclusion seem to provide an adequate ending to the discussion of the topic?
9. Can you think of any questions you could ask the writer that would help improve the draft?
10. Read the draft backwards (starting with the concluding paragraph and ending with the introduction). Do you still feel that each paragraph is connected to the one preceding it?

Student Draft

Here is a student draft. Read it and compare it with your own draft. In the margin, write a short summary of the main idea of each paragraph. Then write a one-paragraph summary at the end.

Bilingual Education

1 I think bilingual education is necessary in the United States, because the immigrants are growing every day. Being bilingual, we can have more opportunities to go ahead in the United States. Children and adults who are English speaking are affected by bilingualism in this country also.

2 Every day, the number of immigrants in this country grows. They came from other countries where they don't know English. Most of the immigrants came from Spanish or Asian native languages and they bring their children with them also. People like them know that it is necessary to learn English because the United States is English.

3 Last year an immigrant with Spanish native language went to see the doctor. He did not know how to explain to his doctor his problem and his doctor spoke only English. Since it was a waste of time to be with the doctor, he went back to his house and got even sicker.

4 Furthermore, being a bilingual person would enable an individual to get better opportunities for bilingual secretaries, for example. You can see them in the ads in the newspaper. There is a program at Hostos Community College of the City University of New York which will help develop both job skills and bilingual training.

5 Children speak their native language because that is the language they hear their parents speak. These children are affected

psychologically when they go to their first year of classes in a school where only English is spoken. The children feel a great deal of stress listening to words that they do not understand. This frustration gives them a reason to drop out of school.

6 If the same children were enrolled in a bilingual education program, they would be able to stay on grade level while they learned English. I have a nephew who is in third grade and is making good grades both in English and in his content courses taught in Spanish. Next year he will exit out of the program and take all his courses in English. Though he will still have to continue to improve his English skills, he is far better off than if he were thrown into the middle of an English-speaking school where he would learn to think of himself as a failure.

7 In the United States, in some places they discriminate against a person who does not know English, giving them a low position of work, paying them $3 an hour. Sometimes they do not give them a job. This discrimination sometimes helps inspire the job seeker to work harder at learning English.

8 I agree with bilingual education in the United States because the same country gives immigrants the right to be in this country knowing that they will arrive not knowing English. The Constitution says that people should all have equal chance in education. Bilingual education is a valid method to give equal opportunities to people of other languages and cultures.

▶WRITING FOCUS: Improving Coherence

In good writing, ideas should flow from sentence to sentence and from paragraph to paragraph.

Look at the preceding draft. Notice how abruptly the writer goes from the point about job training (paragraph 4) and opportunities to the point about children's education (paragraph 5). Then the writer jumps from the topic of children's education back to ideas that focus on careers (paragraph 7). Where is the thesis? That is, what is the writer's main idea? How and where is it supported? How could the transitions be written differently in order to enable the reader to follow more easily?

One way would be to reorganize the sequence of paragraphs so that paragraph 7 follows paragraph 4 since they both focus on adults and bilingual education. A transition phrase at the beginning of the point about children would help improve coherence. With your teacher's help, try to think of one, such as, "Adults are not the only ones who can benefit from bilingual education."

Now look at sentences in the paragraphs and see if each one leads smoothly to the next. There are key words that can assist with connecting ideas between sentences, such as *this, that, it*. By using these pronouns to refer back to an idea presented in a previous sentence, you make sure that there is an "idea bridge" from one sentence to the next. Repeating a key word that names the main idea, such as the word "education" in paragraph 8, accomplishes the same thing.

Now, examine the other paragraphs and sentences to see if you can find ways to improve the flow of ideas. Then revise the student essay, making it more coherent.

Now, reread your draft aloud. Examine it to see if you can improve the "connectedness" or coherence.

Compare the following newspaper article by Dr. Barbara Mujica with the student draft you just examined. Which is more coherent? Why?

BILINGUALISM'S GOAL

by Professor Barbara Mujica, Georgetown University

1 Mine is a Spanish-speaking household. We use Spanish exclusively. I have made an effort not only to encourage use of the language but also to familiarize my children with Hispanic culture. I use books from Latin America to teach them to read and write, and I try to maintain close contacts with Spanish-speaking relatives. Instilling in my children a sense of ethnic identity is my role; it is not the role of the school system. The public schools have the responsibility to teach skills needed in public life—among them the use of the English language. I differ with educators who advocate bilingual education programs whose goal is to preserve the Spanish language and culture among children of Hispanic families.

2 These professionals argue that in an English-speaking environment, Spanish-speaking children often feel alienated and that this causes them to become withdrawn and hostile. Imagine how much more alienated these youngsters will feel if they are kept in special programs.

3 Hispanics, counted at 14.6 million in the 1980 census, may number 47 million by the year 2020. Yet they are notoriously underrepresented in the arts, sciences, professions, and politics. Economically, as a group, they tend to lag.

4 To get better jobs, young people must be fluent in English. Without English, they will be unable to protest to the proper authorities if they are abused. Non-English-speaking individuals are vulnerable to not only economic but also political exploitation.

5 The goal of bilingual education must be the mainstreaming of non-English-speaking children through the teaching of English. Ethnic identity, like religion, is a family matter.

EXERCISE 7: Coherence

1. Summarize Mujica's essay.
2. Which draft is better, Mujica's or the student's? Tell why.
3. Read aloud the "idea bridges" Mujica used to go from one idea to the other.

▶ **SCREENING ROOM**

The movie *Stand and Deliver* tells the powerful true story of Jaime Escalante, a high school teacher in the barrio of East Los Angeles, and his Hispanic students. Their accomplishments together, against great odds, make an inspiring account. Edward James Olmos gives a moving performance as the remarkable, dedicated educator. *Stand and Deliver* (1987) is available at most video stores.

EXERCISE 8: Thinking About the Movie

1. Write a brief summary of the events of the film.
2. What did you learn about education in the United States that you did not know?
3. How did the movie change any of your views on education?

▶Editing: Subordinate Clauses

In Chapter Two we studied compound sentences. These sentences express two ideas that are of equal importance. Many times when you write, however, you will want to express ideas that are not of equal importance or weight. Then, one sentence will become a *subordinate clause*. For example:

When their son graduated from college, the parents were filled with joy.

In the sentence above, the main idea (the focus of the sentence) is "the parents were filled with joy." Notice that, if the rest of the sentence were erased,

The parents were filled with joy.

would still be a complete sentence. The part that says

When their son graduated from college,

is there because it tells something about the main part. It tells when they "were filled with joy." That is, the first part (or clause) describes the second clause.

The part that can stand on its own, the main part, is called the independent clause. The part that modifies or describes is called the dependent or subordinate clause.

In this case, because the subordinate clause modifies the verb (that is, it tells *when* something was done), it is acting as an adverb; therefore, the clause is an adverbial subordinate clause, or adverb clause. Such modifying clauses are often introduced with adverbial conjunctions, such as the following:

after	how	though	wherever
although	if	unless	whether
as far as	now that	until	while
as if	since	when	
before	so that	whenever	
even though	than	where	

(Be sure you know the meanings of all these words. If there is one with which you are not familiar, look it up, and learn it.)

These words and phrases most often act as conjunctions that lead into adverb subordinate clauses. There are, however, exceptions. Sometimes some of these words could introduce an adjective clause. For example:

The time *when* we were young seemed short.

In this sentence, the words *when we were young* act as an adjective clause, modifying the noun *time*; the independent clause is *The time... seemed short*. More often than not, however, the words in the list above signal the beginning of an adverbial clause, one that tells where, when, or how something is done.

EXERCISE 9: Finding Subordinate Clauses That Are Adverbs

1. Reread paragraph 2 of Mujica's editorial.
2. Give an example of an adverbial clause in the essay.
3. How many adverbial clauses are in the essay? In your own composition?
4. Select five of the adverbial conjunctions from the list on this page and make up a sentence for each.

Placement of a Subordinate Clause in a Sentence

There are actually a variety of ways of joining the subordinate clause "After they learn English" with the main clause

"Immigrants can get a good job." The first two ways are obvious, but there are others.

1. After they learn English, immigrants can get a good job.
2. Immigrants can get a good job after they learn English.
3. Immigrants, after they learn English, can get a good job.

Each of these examples is completely acceptable—even number 3 in which the main clause is split up by the subordinate clause. Note that the main clause is still "Immigrants can get a good job" and the subordinate clause is still "After they learn English." Having a choice of sentence structures enables you to be more flexible and your writing to be more interesting to read.

EXERCISE 10: Punctuating Subordinate Clauses Correctly

Look at paragraph 2 of Mujica's article on page 52. In the last sentence are the words:

if they are kept in special programs

If those words were alone, and began with a capital letter, would that be a complete sentence?

In the following, identify the sentence fragments, and make them into complete sentences.

1. After they learn English. Immigrants can get a good job.
2. We practiced writing in English. When the course began.
3. The most qualified applicants were hired immediately. If they knew English.
4. Whenever we try to learn French in France. People are very friendly.
5. They conversed in groups. While the teacher conferred with each individual about his English writing.

EXERCISE 11: Correcting Punctuation of Subordinate Clauses

Rewrite the following paragraphs correctly. When you are finished, circle each adverb subordinate clause.

Yu-an just arrived in the New York Harbor. When the fireworks display of Fourth of July went off in the sky. She looked up in amazement.

While her brother cried by her side. He was thinking of his relatives back in China.

Soon her mother and father came back from gathering the luggage and after they said good by to their friends, the family went to the street to find transportation to their new home. Suddenly her father stopped and looked off in the distance. Because someone was shouting his name. He was happy to see his new American friend, David.

Editing often involves using correct "sentence boundaries," or punctuation. The following criteria apply to complete sentences in English:

1. The sentence must have a subject and a verb.
2. The sentence must make a complete thought independent of the context. (If the sentence is written on a piece of paper by itself, will it make sense?)
3. The sentence must end with a period [.], a question mark [?], or an exclamation point [!].

EXERCISE 12: Error Analysis

1. Check your draft to find out if the punctuation is correct according to the preceding rules. Be particularly careful to check sentences with subordinate clauses.
2. Read your draft aloud to the class.
3. Ask someone who has a different point of view to read his or her draft. Compare the two; how are they different and how are they alike?
4. Now, form groups and try to role-play the opposite point of view from that which you took in your composition. If you argued *for* bilingual education, pretend you are *against* it. Set up your reasons why, and your evidence. Then write an argument essay that is the opposite of the one you just wrote. Hand in your draft to the instructor.

▶Writing with Time, Topic, and Audience Constraints

EXERCISE 13: Writing a Timed Essay

Although English is clearly the dominant language of the United States, there is no legal or Constitutional "official language" of the country. There is currently, however, a growing movement in the U.S.

that would make English the "Official Language." Some proposed laws seek to make it illegal for any language other than English to be used in public functions (on election ballots, in schools, etc.). Such laws, which some people call unconstitutional (and even racist), have been passed in a handful of states, while similar legislation is pending in others. Other people counter that English is undeniably the native language of the United States, and to state that legally would only confirm what is already known; furthermore, to have everyone agree on the use of English would be better for the country's progress and that of her citizens.

Do you agree or disagree that English should be the official language of the United States? Does this (or any) country *need* an official language? Why or why not?

In one hour, write an essay arguing your opinion on this topic. Pretend that it will be submitted to the leading newspaper of the city or town in which you live. (In fact, if you are satisfied with it, why not submit it to the newspaper? There is hardly a community in the United States where this topic is not a newsworthy issue.)

Here's how to start:

1. Decide what your opinion is.
2. Make a list of ideas that you want to include.
3. With a pen that has erasable ink for quick corrections, take the point you want to make and write an introductory paragraph.
4. In paragraphs 2 and 3 give reasons why, with examples, illustration, and evidence, factual or anecdotal.
5. Write a concluding paragraph which summarizes, analyzes, and concludes your position. When your time limit is up, hand in the essay you just wrote to your instructor for evaluation.

CHAPTER ▸FOUR

Sexism: Inequality in the Workplace

▸Prewriting

In many cultures, there is a male power base that keeps women "in their place" and does not allow them to compete on an equal basis with men. In this country, affirmative action that blossomed in the 60s has improved the status of women somewhat, providing opportunities for women where none existed before. Discrimination, however, is still rampant in our society, particularly in some career areas, such as the military.

Can you think of any other areas of life in which sexism (the exploitation and domination of one sex by the other)[1] is still taking place? Remember that sexism can include discrimination against men by women, although this is much less common.

[1] Webster's New World Dictionary.

EXERCISE 1: Cluster Diagram

Make a cluster diagram on the topic "sexism." This will help you with the following exercise.

EXERCISE 2: Thinking About the Issue

In groups or pairs, discuss and write the answers to the following:

1. What is the meaning of sexism in today's society?
2. Name instances in which members of your group experienced sexist attitudes at school, at work, or in public.
3. If given a second chance, how would you resolve some of the problems discussed in item 2?
4. How do attitudes toward the sexes differ in this country from those in your native country? How do they differ in the workplace?
5. How is sexism like racism and other prejudices? How do they differ?

▶Reading Selection

The following article, regarding the problem of sexual discrimination in employment, was published in *U.S. News & World Report* in 1991. The "glass ceiling" is a metaphor that describes the unseen barriers that prevent women from advancing beyond certain levels in the professional arena.

Trouble at the Top

A U.S. survey says a "glass ceiling" blocks women from corporate heights. New critics say it's time for women to re-examine their goals.

by Amy Saltzman

1 The ammunition for the next big battle between the sexes lies on Labor Secretary Lynn Martin's desk. Dubbed the "glass ceiling **initiative**," the controversial study on gender discrimination in the executive suite has been deep-sixed[1] since its March due date. With luck, say department insiders, recommendations finally may emerge "sometime this summer."

---

[1]deep-six: to throw overboard; figuratively, to get rid of.

2 On the face of it, the survey of nine major companies, including PepsiCo and Sterling Drug, contains little to justify this cloak-and-dagger secrecy. The report concludes that women's routes to the top are blocked by a "glass ceiling" of subtle discrimination that limits their opportunities to participate in everything from overseas assignments to company-sponsored training programs. Misconceptions about what women want also **hamper** their progress. At many of the companies studied, for example, men in positions of authority often assumed that a woman who had children wouldn't be interested in a high profile transfer or change of assignment because of the longer hours the job would require.

3 **A lousy 3 percent.** Such subtle discrimination is one reason the glass ceiling has remained a rigid barrier for women attempting to push beyond middle management. Today, 3 of every 100 top executive jobs, on average, at the largest U.S. companies are held by women, according to a study by the University of California at Los Angeles Graduate School of Management and corporate **recruiter** Korn/Ferry International—a number that has barely **budged** in a decade.

4 But beyond its actual findings, the significance of the Labor Department's glass-ceiling report lies in the **aura** of indecision and **ambivalence** that surrounds it. Secretary Martin has told aides she won't release the findings of the report until she can devise recommendations that will help women break through the glass ceiling—and in the Bush administration, selling any kind of antidiscrimination remedy won't be easy. Others on the Bush team have wanted the report kept under wraps for fear that it could hurt their case against some provisions of the **pending** civil rights act. Indeed, the White House strongly opposes part of the bill that passed in the House last week: It would allow women to seek **punitive** damages in discrimination cases. "There is some nervousness about how the glass-ceiling initiative will be interpreted and what kind of enforcement effort will be required," says one Labor Department official. "Certainly it helps us if we can distance it from the civil rights debate."

5 Caught in the crossfire are many of the 56 million women in the workforce. Nearly 30 years after feminist pioneer Betty Friedan

called on women to emerge from their suburban prisons and join men in the world of work, feminism has yet to square its own goals with the burdens of equality—most notably, the long hours necessary to succeed in certain careers and the financial and emotional costs of putting kids in day care. As political and corporate leaders **grapple** for solutions, a whole new group of feminists are calling for nothing short of a complete **overhaul** of the women's movement. These neofeminists argue that the glass ceiling itself represents one more futile attempt by women to seek equality under a system of rules, laws, and policies created by men, for men. Instead, they **advocate** remodeling the workplace along less hierarchical, more "female" lines.

6 **A new strategy.** These critics insist they are not calling for a halt in the fight for equal opportunity but merely for a rethinking of the game plan. And they carry some powerful ammunition: For most women—not simply those who have failed to break through the glass ceiling—true equality remains **elusive.** More than 60 percent of women in the work force are **mired** in low-paying clerical and sales jobs. The pay gap between men and women is still yawning.[2] Overall, women now earn just 72 cents for every dollar a man takes home, compared with 64 cents 10 years ago—not much progress since Moses decreed that a man between 20 and 60 was worth 50 silver shekels, while a woman of the same age was worth just 30 shekels.

7 Some women are simply ditching the race to the executive suite because the closer they move to the top, the less certain they become that the **pinnacle** of the men's world is the worthiest of goals. "After two decades of clinging to the male model, there has been an exploding of the notion that career achievement and material rewards are the yardsticks of life," observes economist Sylvia Ann Hewlett, author of *A Lesser Life—The Myth of Women's Liberation in America.*

8 That was certainly the case for Robin Schirmer, a 38-year-old attorney from Chicago. Torn between raising her 4-year-old son herself and putting in the 10-to-15-hour days necessary to be

[2]yawning: [figurative] opening or growing wider.

judged a success in her profession, she gave up a **lucrative** downtown law practice three years ago to open a small suburban firm with two other female attorneys. Schirmer's income is now less than a third of her previous salary in the high five figures, but she has the flexibility she craved and time to spend with her family. "I think a lot of us realized that we overemphasized the importance of career in achieving equality," she says.

9 **Bailing out.** Some women are going a step further than Schirmer and bailing out of the workforce altogether. The percentage of women in the workforce ages 20 to 44 dropped between June and December of last year, from 74.5 percent to 74 percent—the largest decrease since the early '60s. This percentage, which remained unchanged in the first quarter of 1991, is significant, economists say, because it appears to be coupled with a sea change[3] in attitudes and behavior. Fertility rates have shot up 10.5 percent since 1985: Last year's 4.2 million births constituted the highest rate since the baby boom year of 1963.

10 Nearly 30 percent of working women polled last year by the Connecticut research firm Yankelovich Clancy Shulman said that "wanting to put more energy into being a good homemaker and mother" was a reason to consider giving up work indefinitely—an 11 percent increase over 1989 and the highest such figure in 20 years. Moreover, in a survey of 1,000 career professionals conducted by the executive recruiting firm Robert Half International, 82 percent of the women polled said they would choose a career path with flexible full-time work hours and more family time, but slower career advancement over one with inflexible hours and faster advancement. And the number of women who bucked the system and chose to start their own businesses reached an all-time high last year of 3.1 million, a 50 percent increase over 1980.

11 Perhaps the sharpest break between these new advocates and their **predecessors** is a view that true equality can be achieved only if the differences between men and women are valued equally. For some, that means reemphasizing women's traditional care-giving role in the home. For others, it implies putting a greater focus on

[3] sea change: [figurative] a gradual shift.

integrating "feminine" qualities like nurturing and sharing into the workplace. Nowhere is the clash more evident than in the legal field where feminist attorneys are calling for a rethinking of laws from a "woman's perspective."

12 These new feminist leaders point to the recent U.S. Supreme Court decision in *United Automobile Workers v. Johnson Controls* as a classic example of how the narrow quest for individual rights has led the women's movement astray. In that case, the justices ruled that excluding women of childbearing age from jobs that could damage their fetuses constituted a civil rights violation. But the apparent "victory" left some feminists squirming. "Now women, as well as men, have the right to work in a dangerous workplace," observes Ruth Rosen, a professor of history at the University of California at Davis who is writing a book on contemporary American feminism. "What kind of victory is that?"

13 **Reinventing the workplace.** While high-court decisions grab headlines, the most significant battles are taking place behind closed office doors and on factory floors. Partly as a result of the steady hemorrhage[4] of female talent, corporations are finding that they must go beyond **piecemeal** programs like flextime[5] and day care and rethink their assumptions about what constitutes a truly supportive work environment. Even companies that win awards for enlightened work and family policies have made little progress in bringing women into the upper ranks. In *Working Mother* magazine's most recent list of the top 75 companies for women, fewer than 10 percent of officers or vice presidents in 48 of the firms were female.

14 Management consultant Marilyn Loden thinks she knows why. Loden, the author of *Workforce America!,* a new book on managing in a diverse workplace, argues that women would prosper if they were encouraged to use what numerous studies have shown to be their generally stronger **intuitive** and people skills instead of adopting the "male" command-and-control style. When she began promoting that idea several years ago, it drew nothing but barbs

---

[4]hemorrhage: heavy bleeding; [figurative] a flowing away of an important resource.

[5]flextime: a business policy which allows employees to create work schedules to accommodate their other responsibilities.

from women and men who thought "focusing on differences would reinforce stereotypes and prevent women from getting ahead."

15 **Vive la difference.** Today, as the pool of skilled white male workers shrinks and **demographic** shifts create an ethnically diverse workforce, more companies are starting to listen to Loden and her followers. Du Pont, NYNEX, PepsiCo, and Lotus Development Corp. are among the firms that have instituted programs aimed at helping employees understand and value the differences between men and women. Though the programs are still young, some executives say they are pleased with the changes they have wrought. Steve Bottcher, vice-president of operations for PepsiCo, went through a 3 1/2 day diversity-training course and said afterwards: "A year ago I might have automatically hired somebody who thought like me. Now I am much more likely to hire someone with a different point of view." At software maker Lotus, all staffers are required to attend a diversity-training course in which they discuss, among other things, why men often ignore women who speak during meetings and how showing emotions, even crying in the office, can indicate a deep commitment to the job.

16 Such group gropes[6] are not as hokey[7] as they might seem. Indeed, a growing body of scientific and social research supports the notion that in work—as in love and play—men and women experience and react to the world differently. In her new book, *Brain Sex: The Real Difference Between Men and Women,* British **geneticist** Anne Moir contends that in the guise of political correctness, science has down-played the gender-specific differences of the brain itself. She cites numerous studies showing, for example, that men have fewer fibers connecting the verbal and emotional areas of the brain, making it more difficult for them to express emotions. By contrast, males demonstrate a superior ability to understand abstract relationships, which may make them

[6]group grope: [slang] an informal idea-generating session among an assembly of people.

[7]hokey: [slang] corny; trite; outdated.

more naturally suited to disciplines such as mathematics and engineering.

17 **Power lunches.** Whether the behavior is **innate** or learned, a raft of psychological studies indicate that women are more focused on intimacy and making connections with other people, while men are more centered on autonomy, power, and asserting independence. In her current best-seller, *You Just Don't Understand: Women and Men in Conversation,* linguist Deborah Tannen makes that **dichotomy** the centerpiece of her analysis of sex differences in conversation. Men, for instance, often talk more easily in public before a group of people than with their spouses or girlfriends at the dinner table. Tannen's explanation: In a public setting, a man feels challenged to demonstrate his intelligence and expertise, whereas at home he has nothing to prove and no one to defend against—and therefore no reason to talk. For women, of course, those dinner conversations form the crucial bonds of intimacy that make or break a relationship.

18 Outside the home, such thinking has triggered efforts to reemphasize the contributions of women as nurturers. In her new book *Prisoners of Men's Dreams,* feminist writer Suzanne Gordon contends that the current shortfalls in areas like child care and health care are rooted in the "ambivalent attitude toward caring and the caring professions displayed by equal-opportunity feminism." She calls on the feminist movement and women in high-powered careers to "end their assault" on those who choose careers in such fields as nursing, teaching, and social work. To drive her point home, Gordon has formed a National Care Coalition made up of people in the care-giving professions to lobby for national day care, health care, and elderly care.

19 Not all neofeminists believe it is up to society to change, however. Historian Camille Paglia, author of the controversial book, *Sexual Personae,* argues that women have to make a choice: either to adapt to the male standard of success, which she credits with building great cultures and civilizations, or to seek the rewards that come from raising a family. "By focusing everything on careers, women have given up their greatest power—as child bearers," says Paglia. But most new voices in the women's movement counter

that a real choice is impossible so long as organizations cling to the masculine approach. Indeed, for women hoping for a crack at the chief executive's slot, the choice often is one of following the male model or settling for second best.

Amy Saltzman, "Trouble at the Top," *U.S. News & World Report,* June 17, 1991.

EXERCISE 3: Summarizing

1. Reread the article carefully; then summarize each of the 19 paragraphs in your own words. Write one sentence for each paragraph.
2. Divide into groups. Read aloud your sentence summarizing the first paragraph, until everyone in the group agrees on the main idea of the paragraph. Then proceed to the next paragraph and the next, until they are all done.
3. Now write a one-paragraph summary of the article with your group. Use your summaries of each paragraph.
4. Compare the summaries that each group has written and answer the following questions:
   - **a.** Is any important idea left out?
   - **b.** Are there any details that could be left out?
   - **c.** Did the writer use his or her own words to write the summary?
   - **d.** Does any part of the summary reflect the writer's opinion, rather than the facts of the article?

EXERCISE 4: Thinking About the Reading

With a partner, use the summaries from the preceding exercise and write answers to the following questions.

1. What is the issue presented in this news article?
2. How does the article demonstrate this problem?
3. Why has the problem become a public issue?
4. What steps are being taken to improve the situation that women face in the workplace?
5. How do cultural attitudes influence the behavior of male employers toward female employees?
6. What innate differences between the male and female brain are complicating the issue of equality between sexes?

7. What other underlying problems are complicating the issue?
8. Think about situations you know about that most often lead to sexual harassment—either male or female—and discuss them with the group.
9. Now think about your own solutions to the problem of sexism. Discuss them with your group.

EXERCISE 5: Defining New Words

Define the words highlighted in the article. First, try to guess their meaning from the context. Check your guess with the Glossary at the back of this book. After you have learned the meaning of these words, reread the selection to further your understanding of the new vocabulary words.

Look for other words that are unfamiliar to you. Make a list of them for future reference and keep them in your writing folder.

EXERCISE 6: Vocabulary

advocate	elusive	intuitive	piecemeal
ambivalence	geneticist	lucrative	pinnacle
aura	grapple	mired	predecessors
budged	hamper	overhaul	punitive
demographic	initiative	pending	recruiter
dichotomy	innate		

In each of the sentences below, a word or phrase is italicized. In each case, the italicized word or phrase is a synonym for one of the highlighted vocabulary words in the article by Amy Saltzman. Rewrite the ten sentences below, substituting a synonymous vocabulary word (or form of the word) for the italicized word or phrase.

1. It is difficult enough to succeed in the top ranks of the business world, but for women, sexist attitudes *get in the way of* progress.
2. Because the report was vague and filled with *mixed, unclear meaning,* it was not very useful.
3. Some researchers believe that the attitudes we have about males and females are *with us from birth.*
4. American women in the 1990s have a different approach to attaining their rights than *those who came before them.*
5. It's depressing to be *stuck* in a job, without hope of advancement.
6. There are only a few positions at her firm that are very *high paying.*

7. Anne Moir, who is a *scientist who studies heredity,* asserts that there are basic differences between the sexes.
8. The real reasons that people behave the way they do is *very hard to pin down.*
9. Those attempting to create a workplace that is fair to women *recommend and urge* many changes from the traditional office atmosphere.
10. Trying to change society's attitudes toward women—particularly successful women—in the workplace, one must *struggle* to overcome longstanding prejudices.

EXERCISE 7: Doing Research

1. Go to the periodical section of your library and find at least two sources on the origins of sexual discrimination.
2. Read this information and take notes.
3. Add these notes to those you took from the article in this chapter and those taken during your group discussion work.
4. Come to class ready to participate in a class discussion. Share what you learned in the library with the rest of the class.

▶Writing the Draft

TOPIC: Sexual harassment of females has become an open issue after the sexual revolution became a strong political movement in the 1960s. Many women, encouraged by the feminist movement, have found the courage to make their problem one of public concern. What do you think should be done about sexism in the workplace? Should women be given equal pay for equal work? Should they be given the choice of the same jobs and opportunities for advancement in their jobs as men? Even if they are pregnant? In making your point, be as specific as you can.

1. [for women only] Can you think of any times in your life when you have experienced sexism, that is, when you have been the subject of prejudice because you are female?
2. [for men only] From the male point of view, what (if anything) do you think should be done to achieve equality between the sexes in the workplace?
3. Make an informal list of ideas that you want to include.
4. Start writing your draft, and don't forget to include the main idea in the beginning of the composition.

▶WRITING FOCUS: Know Your Own Bias

Most of us have biases about topics that we have strong feelings about. If you have an opinion that is based on emotion, that is a bias, and you should realize that it does not work in argument. There are some rare cases in which an opinion based on bias or prejudice may be used; however, writers must recognize their own bias, and state to the reader that it is a bias.
For example:

1. *Bias:* Women are not capable of serving in the military; they are not physically strong enough.
   Fact: There are many jobs that women can do ably in the military career area. There is even some evidence that in some physical tasks women have more stamina than men.
2. *Bias:* Women should be home raising children and leave fighting to men.
   Fact: Men can be just as good at nurturing children as women, even though they cannot give birth.

Now, look for examples of bias that weaken your point in your own draft and in the drafts of other members of your writing group. If you have a strong opinion, you may state it in such a way that the reader will know that you are aware that the opinion is not fact, but based on subjective experience.

Another way to evaluate your expression of bias is to imagine someone of the opposite opinion reading your draft. For example, someone who believes in women keeping their traditional role of nurturer may say, "What about the children? Do they suffer from neglect if both parents work?" or "Who makes a home for the family if both parents work?" You have to make your argument convincing to those who disagree. Even if they are not convinced about your view, you should convince them that you have a point of view worth considering, because it is carefully thought through, and not based on emotional bias.
Example:

Women, in my opinion, should be the ones to raise the children, despite the fact that they are physically capable of serving in the military.

►Revising

Divide into groups and read your draft aloud to the members of the group. Get their feedback so that you can start the process of revision.

Divide the group in half and take opposing points of view. Ask a member of each side to take notes on what is said.

Now look at your draft. Did you argue in such a way as to convince the opposition of your point of view? What counter argument could they present to your own argument?

EXERCISE 8: Getting Perspective on Your Own Writing

It is not easy to objectively evaluate your own work when you reread it silently immediately after you've finished writing it. Apply one of the techniques listed below to the draft you just wrote, in order to get "distance" from your own work.

1. Have another student read the essay to you.
2. Tape yourself reading the essay aloud, then listen to the tape.
3. After hearing the essay, read it silently and take notes to identify the portions you may want to change.
4. Put the essay away for a few hours or a few days before you read it again.

EXERCISE 9: Revising Questions

Divide into groups, exchange papers, and apply these questions to the new draft.

1. Is the writer's main idea (his or her "point") stated clearly in the first paragraph?
2. Does each idea and each paragraph follow logically from one to the next? How does each idea *relate* to the one that precedes and follows it?
3. Are all ideas related specifically to the opinion being put forth in this draft? If not, which ones could be eliminated?
4. Which sentences explain, illustrate, or give examples about the topic?
5. What is the main idea of each paragraph? Is the idea adequately explained and developed?
6. Which ideas are particularly interesting? Could you add more details to develop this part of the draft? (Could you have used quotes or other details from the *U.S. News &*

World Report article to support your point? Where should these details be included?)

7. Could a personal anecdote be added to make the argument more convincing? (Use the question words, *Who? What? Where? When? Why? How?* to help you develop your example with specific words.)
8. Does the conclusion seem to provide an adequate ending to your discussion of the topic?
9. Can you think of any questions you could ask the writer that would help in the revision process?
10. Read the draft backwards (from the last paragraph to the first). Do you still feel that each paragraph is connected to the one preceding it?

EXERCISE 10: Evaluating Drafts

Read this student draft. Answer the questions in Exercise 9 as they relate to this draft. How does this writer's discussion of the topic differ from your own? Is the writer's bias present? Is it appropriately or inappropriately expressed?

Student Draft

1 Sexism has become a barrier in the total achievement of a woman's goal in our society today. There is no logical or rational justification for sex prejudice.

2 Women in trying to get a better living for themselves have improved themselves mentally and intellectually and therefore are seeking jobs in areas that pay more and which often are run by men and are trying to compete in areas in which there is constant discrimination.

3 For example, women working in the fire department which has always been a career area for men, they find that they are harassed by male fire fighters who see them as intruders and not fit for the job, so that they are constantly rejected and sexually approached. They also have to stand for harassment in a sexually verbal manner.

4 Women have also been sexually harassed in the military by men who see them as lesbians or militant feminists. They are often denied military promotions because of their sex. Men believe that women should be at home or if recruited should be only as nurses

or behind the line. Women are seen often as the weak sex where they can only compete in a women's world where they are limited.

If we as women give life why shouldn't we be capable of reaching mountains and making ourselves be heard? So I think that women must be recognized as an important group in society. The media must portray women in as positive a manner as possible. If men could see us as people not as sex objects, the world would be a better place to live in.

Now, check this draft with the Revising questions and see what advice could help this writer.

EXERCISE 11: Comparing Two News Articles

1. Find two different news articles on sexual harassment; decide which one is more well written.
2. Evaluate them using the Revising questions.
3. Explain why you prefer one article over the other. What strengths does the better one have? What are the weaknesses of the other one?
4. Now, with a partner or group, compare the pairs of articles and see if you agree or disagree with your classmates.

▶ SCREENING ROOM

Jane Fonda, Lily Tomlin, and Dolly Parton play the parts of female workers sexually harassed, callously abused, and otherwise taken advantage of by their extremely sexist boss, in the 1980 satire, *9 to 5.* Although laughter is the main goal of this movie, it clearly (if broadly) makes some very valid points about the difficulties encountered by women in the workplace. This is a popular title, and should be easy to find in most video rental stores.

EXERCISE 12: Talking About the Movie

1. Write a summary of the events of *9 to 5.*
2. Despite its humorous intent, what message does the movie try to send? Is it successful in communicating that message?

▶Editing: Verbs in the Present Tense

Verbs change form to indicate the time something occurred, is occurring, or will occur. The present tense shows what is or can happen now. To form it, use the root or basic form of the verb. The third person singular [he, she, or it] uses the *s*. For example:

person	**singular**	**plural**
1st person	I *write*	we *write*
2nd person	you *write*	you (plural) *write*
3rd person	he *writes*	they *write*
3rd person	she *writes*	
3rd person	it *writes*	

A common mistake is the leaving off of the *s* from the third person singular, especially when there is an intervening clause or phrase between the subject and the verb.

Correct Example:

The writer, whether she is at home or staying at a hotel, always writes in bed.

Incorrect Example:

The dog sitting under the trees howl at the moon. [Note: the *dog* (singular) howls, not the *trees* (plural)]

EXERCISE 13: Finding Verb Agreement Errors

1. There are many verb agreement errors in the following paragraph. Underline them. Make sure you know the reason that they are errors.

Many articles has been written about how to write a good argument essay. An argument begin with an idea in the mind of the writer, and grow out of an experience in the writer's life. Identifying these ideas and writing them down is not an easy task for most beginning writers. Then, the hard part for many are the development of supporting ideas, illustrations, explanations, and examples. They prefers to stick to generalizations. The interesting thing that occur in the course of writing many compositions, is that writing often enable one to develop the ideas about which one is writing. Although planning is important, insights often comes unexpectedly during the act of writing itself. In fact, writing is a process of continual discovery, examination and experimentation, throughout which ideas are tested, rejected, accepted, retested, and refined.

2. Look at your own draft. Check all the present tense verbs and make sure that they are in agreement with the subject of the sentence. Now hand in your draft to your instructor for evaluation.

▶Writing with Time, Topic, and Audience Constraints

EXERCISE 14: Writing a Timed Essay

Select one of the given topics. Generate an essay within one hour.

Option A: One of the demands of our modern society is that wives work outside the home. Sometimes it is easier for women to find jobs and for men to stay home. This may or may not create problems.What do you think?

Option B: In the Persian Gulf War, many women served in the military, and some were decorated for their bravery in combat. Do you feel that women should be allowed to fight in wars? Write your opinion and be specific.

Option C: Homosexuals in the United States are frequently the object of discrimination in the workplace. Should they be given equal status with heterosexuals? Should all job opportunities that are available to heterosexuals be made available to homosexuals? State your opinion and give reasons.

EXERCISE 15: Reviewing, Revising, and Editing Your Essay

Follow these steps to review, revise, edit, and get the class's feedback.

1. Check for the following:

- Did you complete the essay in one hour?
- Did you get your classmates' feedback?
- Were you able to include a variety of ideas?
- Did you include a personal anecdote?
- Did you write at least four paragraphs (introduction, opinion, illustration, conclusion)?
- Did you correct all misspelled words?
- Did you check your punctuation?
- Are there any subject-verb agreement problems?
- Are the adverbial clauses, if used, correct?

2. Hand in your paper to your instructor for an evaluation.

CHAPTER
▶FIVE

Right to Life?
Right to Choose?

▶Prewriting

Abortion is a controversial issue in the United States. In recent months, many states have passed laws that reverse the 1973 Supreme Court decision that guaranteed a woman's right to decide if she wants to end a pregnancy. People who oppose this right to abortion cite the destruction of fetuses as a crime. Those who support a woman's right to choose point out that what most often becomes of children born of an unwanted pregnancy is more criminal than the destruction of a fetus, and further, that government has no right to regulate any aspect of what a woman chooses to do with her body. How do you feel about this issue?

EXERCISE 1: Understanding Your Own Opinion

1. In a few words, summarize your position on the issue of abortion.
2. Share your summary with a friend. Do you agree or disagree with each other? Give your reasons and use examples from your own observation and/or experience.

▶Reading Selection

Many people are offended by *any* opinion on abortion that differs *at all* from their own. The writers of the following piece, which is excerpted from an article published in *Parade*, attempt a very difficult task: to take a non-emotional, rational look at this most controversial issue, to examine all sides. You will notice that this is an excerpt particularly when you come to the end, because unlike the other argument essays you've read in this book, and unlike the way you've been instructed to write yours, there is no conclusion to this one. It has been intentionally left off. When it is time for you to write your draft, you will call upon the information and argumentation presented in the excerpt, along with further information you will gather in your own research, as well as your own beliefs, opinions, and personal experience. You will make your own point at that time.

Dr. Sagan is a famous science writer and television commentator who teaches and does research at Cornell University. He has received the Pulitzer Prize. Ms. Druyan is secretary of the Federation of American Scientists, a member of the board of directors of the Children's Health Fund in New York City, and a science writer and producer for television. They are married to each other, and they have one child.

Is It Possible to be Pro-Life *and* Pro-Choice?

by Carl Sagan and Ann Druyan [1]

1 Is it wrong to abort a pregnancy? Always? Sometimes? Never? How do we decide? ...In **contemplative** moments, nearly everyone recognizes that the issue is not wholly one-sided. Many **partisans** of differing views, we find, feel some disquiet, some unease when confronting what's behind the opposing arguments. (This is partly why such confrontations are avoided.) And the issue surely touches on deep questions: What are our responsibilities to one another? Should we permit the state to intrude into the most intimate and personal aspects of our lives? Where are the boundaries of freedom? What does it mean to be human?

[1]Reprinted with permission from *Parade*, copyright © 1990.

Testing "Freedom of Choice"

2 Of the many actual points of view, it is widely held—especially in the media, which rarely have the time or the inclination to make fine distinctions—that there are only two: "pro-choice" and "pro-life." This is what the two principal warring camps like to call themselves, and that's what we'll call them here. In the simplest characterization, a pro-choicer would hold that the decision to abort a pregnancy is to be made only by the woman; the state has no right to interfere. And a pro-lifer would hold that, from the moment of conception, the **embryo** or **fetus** is alive; that this life imposes on us a moral obligation to preserve it; and that abortion is **tantamount** to murder. Both names—pro-choice and pro-life—were picked with an eye toward influencing those whose minds are not yet made up: Few people wish to be counted as being against freedom of choice or as opposed to life. Indeed, freedom and life are two of our most cherished values, and here they seem to be in fundamental conflict.

3 Let's consider these two absolutist[1] positions in turn. A newborn baby is surely the same being it was just before birth. There is good evidence that a late-term fetus responds to sound—including music, but especially its mother's voice. It can suck its thumb or do a somersault. Occasionally, it generates adult brain wave patterns. Some people say they remember being born, or even the uterine[2] environment. Perhaps there is thought in the womb. It's hard to maintain that a transformation to full personhood happens abruptly at the moment of birth. Why, then, should it be murder to kill an infant the day after it was born but not the day before?

4 As a practical matter, this isn't very important: less than one percent of all **tabulated** abortions in the United States are listed in the last three months of pregnancy (and, on closer investigation, most such reports turn out to be due to **miscarriage** or miscalculation). But third trimester[3] abortions provide a test of the limits of the pro-choice point of view. Does a woman's "innate right to control her own body" include the right to kill a **near-term** fetus who is, for all intents and purposes, identical to a newborn child?

5 We believe that many supporters of reproductive freedom are troubled at least occasionally by this question. But they are reluctant to raise it because it is the beginning of a slippery slope. If it

---

[1]absolutist: extreme.
[2]uterine: having to do with the womb.
[3]trimester: a period of three months; especially, one of three 3–month periods into which a woman's pregnancy is divided.

is impermissible to abort a pregnancy in the ninth month, what about the eighth, seventh, sixth...? Once we acknowledge that the state can interfere at *any* time in the pregnancy, doesn't it follow that the state can interfere at all times?

6 This conjures up the **specter** of predominantly male, predominantly affluent legislators telling poor women they must bear and raise alone children they cannot afford to bring up; forcing teenagers to bear children they are not emotionally prepared to deal with; saying to women who wish for a career that they must give up their dreams, stay home and bring up babies; and, worst of all, condemning victims of rape and incest to carry and nurture the offspring of their assailants. Legislative prohibitions on abortion arouse the suspicion that their real intent is to control the independence and sexuality of women. Why should legislators have any right at all to tell women what to do with their bodies? To be deprived of reproductive freedom is **demeaning.** Women are fed up with being pushed around.

7 And yet, by **consensus,** all of us think it proper that there be prohibitions against, and penalties exacted for, murder. It would be a flimsy defense if the murderer pleads that this is just between him and his victim and none of the government's business. If killing a fetus is truly killing a human being, is it not the *duty* of the state to prevent it? Indeed, one of the chief functions of government is to protect the weak from the strong.

8 If we do not oppose abortion at *some* stage of pregnancy, is there not a danger of dismissing an entire category of human beings as unworthy of our protection and respect? And isn't that dismissal the **hallmark** of sexism, racism, nationalism and religious **fanaticism?** Shouldn't those dedicated to fighting such injustices be **scrupulously** careful not to embrace another?

Testing the "Right to Life"

9 There is no right to life in any society on Earth today, nor has there been at any former time (with a few rare exceptions, such as among the Jains of India): We raise farm animals for slaughter; destroy forests; pollute rivers and lakes until no fish can live there; kill deer and elk for sport, leopards for their **pelts** and whales for fertilizer; entrap dolphins, gasping and **writhing,** in great tuna nets; club seal pups to death; and render a species **extinct** every day. All these beasts and vegetables are as alive as we. What is (allegedly) protected is not life, but *human* life.

10 And even with that protection, casual murder is an urban commonplace, and we wage "conventional" wars with tolls so terrible that we are, most of us, afraid to consider them very deeply. (Tellingly, state-organized mass murders are often justified by redefining our opponents—by race, nationality, religion or ideology—as less than human.) That protection, that right to life, eluded the 40,000 children under 5 who died on our planet today—as every day—from preventable starvation, **dehydration,** disease and neglect.

11 Those who assert a "right to life" are for (at most) not just any kind of life, but for—particularly and uniquely—human life. So they too, like pro-choicers, must decide what distinguishes a human being from other animals when, during **gestation,** the uniquely human qualities—whatever they are—emerge.

12 Despite many claims to the contrary, life does not begin at conception: It is an unbroken chain that stretches back nearly to the origin of the Earth, 4.6 billion years ago. Nor does *human* life begin at conception: It is an unbroken chain dating back to the origin of our species, tens or hundreds of thousands of years ago. Every human sperm and egg is, beyond the shadow of a doubt, alive. They are not human beings, of course. However, it could be argued that neither is a fertilized egg.

13 In some animals, an egg develops into a healthy adult without benefit of a sperm cell. But not, so far as we know, among humans. A sperm and an unfertilized egg jointly comprise the full genetic blueprint for a human being. Under certain circumstances, after fertilization, they can develop into a baby. But most fertilized eggs are spontaneously[4] miscarried. Development into a baby is by no means guaranteed. Neither a sperm and egg separately, nor a fertilized egg, is more than a *potential* baby or a *potential* adult. So if a sperm and an egg are as human as the fertilized egg produced by their union, and if it is murder to destroy a fertilized egg—despite the fact that it's only *potentially* a baby—why isn't it murder to destroy a sperm or an egg?

14 Hundreds of millions of sperm cells (top speed with tails lashing: 5 inches per hour) are produced in an average human ejaculation[5]. A healthy young man can produce in a week or two enough spermatozoa[6] to double the human population of the Earth. So is masturbation mass murder? How about nocturnal emissions[7] or just plain sex? When the unfertilized egg is expelled each month, has

[4]spontaneously: involuntarily.
[5]ejaculation: discharge of semen.
[6]spermatozoa: sperm; the fertilizing cell of the male.
[7]nocturnal emission: release of sperm during sleep.

someone died? Some lower animals can be grown in the laboratory from a single body cell. If such **cloning** technology were ever developed for humans, would we be committing **genocide** by shedding a drop of blood?

15 All human sperm and eggs are genetic halves of "potential" human beings. Should heroic efforts be made to save and preserve all of them, everywhere, because of this "potential"? Is failure to do so immoral or criminal? Of course, there's a difference between taking a life and failing to save it. And there's a big difference between the probability of survival of a sperm cell and that of a fertilized egg. But the absurdity of a corps of high-minded semen-preservers moves us to wonder whether a fertilized egg's mere "potential" to become a baby really does make destroying it murder.

16 Opponents of abortion worry that, once abortion is permissible immediately after conception, no argument will restrict it at any later time in the pregnancy. Then, they fear, one day it will be permissible to murder a fetus that is unambiguously a human being. Both pro-choicers and pro-lifers (at least some of them) are pushed toward absolutist positions by parallel fears of the slippery slope.

17 Another slippery slope is reached by those pro-lifers who are willing to make an exception in the agonizing case of a pregnancy resulting from rape or incest. But why should the right to live depend on the *circumstances* of conception? If the same child were to result, can the state **ordain** life for the offspring of a lawful union but death for one conceived by force or **coercion?** How can this be just? And if exceptions are extended to such a fetus, why should they be withheld from any other fetus? This is part of the reason some pro-lifers adopt what many others consider the outrageous posture of opposing abortion under any and all circumstances—only excepting, perhaps, when the life of the mother is in danger.

18 By far the most common reason for abortion is birth control. So shouldn't opponents of abortion be handing out contraceptives? That would be an effective way to reduce the number of abortions. Instead, the United States is far behind other nations in the development of safe and effective methods of birth control—and, in many cases, opposition to such research (and to sex education) has come from the same people who oppose abortions...

Carl Sagan and Ann Druyan, "Is It Possible to Be Pro-Life *and* Pro-Choice?" *Parade,* April 22, 1990.

EXERCISE 2: Understanding the Reading

With a partner or group, discuss and write the answers to the following, then share your answers with the other groups in the class.

1. In the excerpt from the article by Sagan and Druyan, the two sides of the abortion issue are discussed. Summarize the two opposing positions in a sentence or two each.
2. Explain, in your own words, the "deep questions" (paragraph 1) that are being asked when one contemplates the issue of abortion.
3. What do the authors mean by the "circumstances of conception" (paragraph 17) under which a child is conceived? How can these have impact on the rightness or wrongness of an abortion?
4. Do you think the authors have an opinion on abortion? What do you think it is, if any? Refer to specific passages in the article that cause you to come to your conclusion. (In other words, "I think Sagan and Druyan believe ____________, because in paragraph 15 they say ____________ ...")

EXERCISE 3: Vocabulary

cloning	embryo	hallmark	scrupulously
coercion	extinct	miscarriage	specter
consensus	fanaticism	near-term	tabulated
contemplative	fetus	ordain	tantamount
dehydration	genocide	partisans	writhing
demeaning	gestation	pelts	

Eleven of the words listed above, all of which were highlighted in the article you just read, are defined below. Match the words to the appropriate definitions.

1. n., the period of carrying developing offspring in a mother's womb; pregnancy. ____________
2. adj., no longer existing in living form. ____________
3. n., the systematic, planned annihilation of a racial, political, or cultural group. ____________
4. n., the first stage of development of any organism; figuratively, the earliest stage of anything, such as an idea. ____________
5. n., the later stage of development of certain animals within the womb (in a human, beginning after the 8th week after conception). ____________

6. adj., thoughtful; meditative. ___________
7. n., the early, involuntary expulsion of a nonviable fetus in mid-pregnancy. ___________
8. n., any indication of quality or excellence. ___________
9. n., the act of forcing someone to act or think in a given manner. ___________
10. n., the act of drying or removing all the water from something. ___________
11. n., non-sexual reproduction of identical offspring of plants or animals from a single cell of the "parent." ___________

After you have determined the vocabulary word to match each of the eleven definitions, use them (or formations of them) to complete the following sentences.

1. Marine biologists and ecologists are determined to save the humpback whale, which has been hunted almost out of existence, from ___________.
2. After spending several days in the desert without any supplies, the soldier was almost completely ___________.
3. Human beings and orangutans have a ___________ period lasting about nine months; a hamster's is only 16 days, while that of an elephant lasts more than 20 months!
4. Medical science has developed equipment which enables doctors to examine an ___________ in the uterus only a week or two after conception.
5. Having suffered a ___________ during her first pregnancy, Elizabeth was reluctant to try again.
6. Using an excellent vocabulary is one of the ___________ of a fine writer.
7. She was reluctant to have an abortion when the ___________ was nearly fully developed.
8. I was in a ___________ mood, quietly thinking about everything that had happened.

9. The prisoner was ___________ by his brutal captors into signing a false confession.
10. The biologist attempted to ___________ a new frog from a single cell of another one.
11. The Ibo tribe of Nigeria was almost completely wiped out in the 1960s in a brutal government effort that can only be described as attempted ___________.

EXERCISE 4: Doing Research on a Topic

Because the issue of abortion is such a complex one, some factual research is called for. Divide into three groups, numbered 1, 2, and 3. Each person in Group 1 should go to the library and find information *from at least three different sources* on Topic A below; each person in Group 2 should gather information from *at least three different sources* on Topic B; and each person in Group 3 should gather information from at least three different sources on Topic C.

Come back together and share your work with your group members, and then with the whole class.

Topic A: Roe vs. Wade, the landmark 1973 decision by the Supreme Court on abortion

Topic B: The stages of prenatal development

Topic C: Recent legislative decisions on abortion

On a separate sheet of paper, write how the information you found relates to your position on abortion. Has your position changed or is it the same?

▶Writing the Draft

EXERCISE 5: Choosing Your Topic

Of the four positions on abortion that follow, choose one for the topic of an argument essay, and make your point.

1. Abortion after the instant of conception is murder. No abortion is ever permissible.
2. A woman has the right to choose abortion any time during pregnancy.

3. Abortions should be permitted within the first three months of pregnancy.
4. Abortion should be permitted within the first six months of pregnancy.

Defend your opinion, using specific facts, clearly presented evidence, and logical argumentation. You may also compare two of these positions, and explain which one you prefer.

▶Revising

EXERCISE 6: Evaluating a Draft

1. Read the following student draft and compare it with your own.
2. How does this writer develop her thesis statement?
3. Is she convincing? How would you change the way she responded to the topic (without changing her opinion)?
4. How coherent is the writer? Explain with examples from the text.

Student Draft

Abortion

1 In my opinion, abortion is morally wrong. I could only accept abortion if the mother or the fetus' life is in danger. Furthermore abortion has failed to solve society's problem, and it has become a legal and social issue that is divisive for our society.

2 Though the abortion is an abuse on the defenseless creature, some mothers do not kill the fetus. Instead they make life a living nightmare for the child after it is born. Some of these mothers actually try to kill the baby by putting it in the garbage. At times, if the mother is too immature, the child is neglected badly.

3 The homeless situation is a problem for poor unwed mothers. I work in a homeless shelter and I see many examples of poor parenting due to frustration of being homeless. Homelessness is a problem not being faced by our society.

4 On the other hand, women should not use abortion as a form of birth control. There are many means to avoid getting pregnant and women have the opportunity to become educated in ways to prevent getting pregnant. In my opinion, abortion should be decided on a case-by-case method.

▶Writing Focus: Avoiding Over-simplification in Argument

As we have seen in this chapter, abortion is a very complicated issue. Therefore when you write your composition on the topic, you should avoid making a very complicated issue seem simple.

If you make a point, you must qualify it by making clear the part of the issue you are including and speak to that issue only; you must let the reader know you are not including all parts of the issue. For example:

1. Women who have abortions suffer painful emotional reactions.
2. Abortions are always appropriate when the child was conceived accidentally.
3. Abortion is the only sensible method of birth control.
4. A person who has an abortion is not a religious person.
5. People who have abortions have no regard for human life.

EXERCISE 7: Avoiding Oversimplifications

1. Based on what you have learned about the complicated nature of the issue, why are the five statements in Writing Focus oversimplification?
2. Write the counter-argument that would disqualify each statement. Could facts be found to support these counter-arguments?
3. Write the statements in a more believable, less oversimplified, less biased way. For example, for number 1 you might write:

Although some women are depressed after having an abortion, others experience only a minor physical discomfort.

EXERCISE 8: Revising Questions

Apply these revising questions to the student draft on page 86, and then to your own draft.

1. Is the writer's main idea (his or her "point") stated clearly in the first paragraph?
2. Does each idea and each paragraph follow logically from one to the next? How does each idea *relate* to the one that precedes and follows it?

3. Are all ideas related specifically to the opinion being put forth in this draft? If not, which ones could be eliminated?
4. Which sentences explain, illustrate, or give examples about the topic?
5. What is the main idea of each paragraph? Is the idea adequately explained and developed?
6. Which ideas are particularly interesting? Could the writer add more details to develop this part of the draft? (Could the writer have used information found in the Sagan/Druyan article to support one or more of his statements? Where should these details be included?)
7. Could a personal anecdote be added to make the argument more convincing? (Use the question words, *Who? What? Where? When? Why? How?* to help you develop your example with specific words.)
8. Does the conclusion seem to provide an adequate ending to the discussion of the topic?
9. Can you think of any questions that you could ask the writer that would help in the revision process?
10. Read the draft backwards (from the last paragraph to the first). Do you still feel that each paragraph is connected to the one preceding it?

▶ SCREENING ROOM

If you wish to see an interesting and well-acted dramatization about the people and events involved in the famous Supreme Court abortion decision known as Roe vs. Wade, there is a 1989 film available on video, called simply *Roe vs. Wade*. Holly Hunter plays "Jane Roe" (a generic name given to protect her identity); Amy Madigan plays Sarah Weddington, the lawyer who argued the case, first in Texas and then all the way to the U.S. Supreme Court.

EXERCISE 9: Thinking About the Movie

1. What (if any) biases do you think are held by the people who wrote and directed this movie?
2. Describe the two main characters in the film. How are they different? What do they have in common?

▶Editing

EXERCISE 10: Verb Tense and Consistency

As we have discussed before, verbs have tense markers which tell the time in which an action is occurring. In English there are several ways of expressing past tense. The most common are:

1. The **simple past tense**

   This is usually expressed with a past tense ending; by far the most common of these is *-ed*. It tells about an action completed at a specific time in the past. The *simple past* tense often occurs with an adverb stating when the action took place. For example:

   She learn*ed* about her father *yesterday.*

   There are many verbs in which the simple past tense is formed irregularly (that is, not by adding the suffix *-ed*), for example:

   The woman *brought* the birth certificate to the lawyer.

   For a complete list of irregular simple past tense verbs, refer to Appendix 2.

2. The **past progressive**

   This shows continuous past action. It is sometimes interrupted by another action. For example:

   The woman *was giving* birth when the news announcement was made about international disarmament.

3. The **present perfect**

   This is formed by using the auxiliary *has* (third person singular only) or *have* (all other cases) with the past participle of the verb. It is used to express past action begun in the past and continuing into the present. For example:

   The child *has known* her real father's name all along.

   (That is, she found out his name in the past and she still knows it.)

4. The **past perfect**

   Create this by using the auxiliary *had* and the past participle of the verb. It is used to denote past action begun in the past and completed in the past. For example:

She *had known* the truth even before that terrible day.

There are additional exercises with verb tenses in the Appendix.

When you are writing a composition, you must express tense correctly to denote time. Do not change the tense without intending to change the meaning of time.

EXERCISE 11: Tense Consistency

In the following paragraphs, correct the inconsistency errors in tense.

Wati knew who her real father was long before anyone told her. She had found an old letter in the attic in which her mother told her sister about a visit to a doctor who is going to find a sperm donor and perform artificial insemination. It is shortly after this date that Wati have been born. Wati's mother marries a man who is her stepfather after she was born.

Instead of the truth, she is learning that her father had died in World War II. She had seen pictures of a man who she will think was her father. Who is that man? Wati is deciding that she will confront her mother. That is last year. Now, she thought she told her mother what she discovers that fateful day last October.

Now, examine your draft. Are there any verb tenses inappropriately used?

►Writing With Time, Topic, and Audience Constraints

Abortion is a very old medical procedure, and the argument over the morality of it is also old. Sometimes progress raises new moral questions. Modern technology has in recent years enabled women who had been unable to become pregnant through "normal" means to do so by means of *artificial insemination*. In this process, a man donates his sperm under laboratory conditions, and the sperm is then implanted in the woman's womb. Once done by a couple who could not have a baby any other way, this is also done today through "sperm banks," wherein anonymous men, motivated only by payment, donate healthy sperm, which is later used to impregnate a woman. In this case, the mother and "father" do not know each other at all.

Artificial insemination has also led to another late 20th century innovation, the *surrogate mother*. In this case, a couple who want to have a child, but who cannot because the wife is infertile, employ a woman to accomplish what the wife cannot. The surrogate mother agrees, generally for a fee, to be artificially inseminated by the husband, to become pregnant, to carry and deliver the child, and then allow the man and his wife to be the father and adoptive mother of the child.

These relatively new practices naturally raise a host of legal and moral issues. If you wish to do research you will find that thousands of articles and books have been written on these topics. An article in the *New York Daily News* reports on issues brought forward during an attempt by a woman to find her biological (her actual, as opposed to her adoptive) father. Such questions as the screening of sperm donors and the responsibility of the donor to the offspring have yet to be answered. Another question is whether or not the offspring of artificial insemination should be fully informed of the facts of their conception, including the identity of the biological father (the sperm donor). Other questions: What is the definition of a father? Is it always the person whose sperm fertilized the egg? What about the adoptive father who gave nurturancc, support, and love, but not sperm? What about the mother who gives her child up for adoption? And what about the child's rights, particularly the rights of the grown child who is curious about his or her biological background?

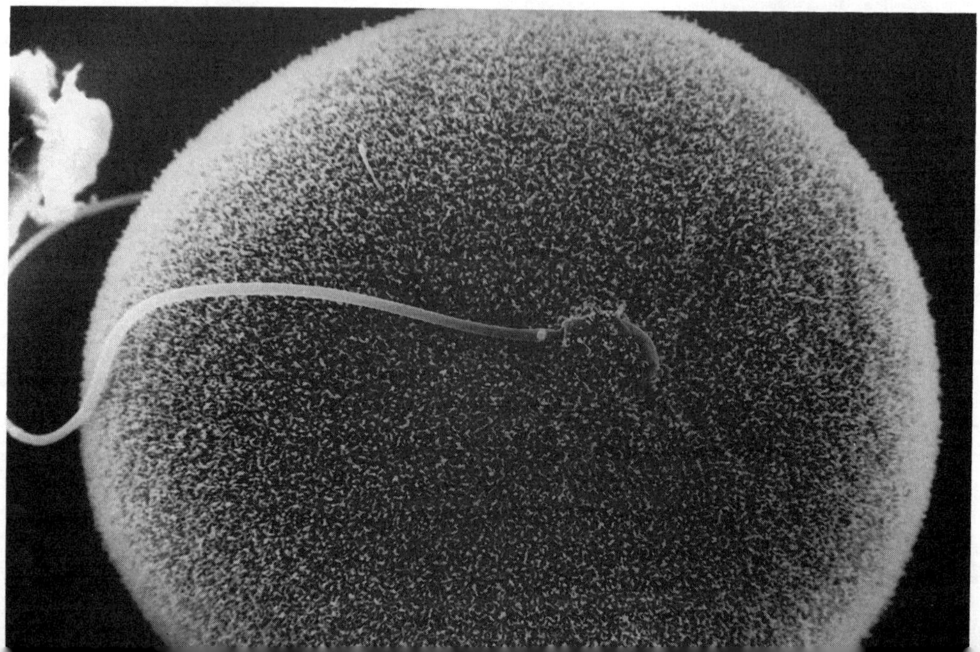

EXERCISE 12: Writing a Timed Essay

Write a draft in one hour arguing pro or con on one of the issues raised in the preceding paragraph. Assume that the audience for your argument essay is your writing class.

When you are finished, read it over. Now, write a new essay on the same topic, but choose one of the two audiences listed below and assume that now the draft must be written for them:

1. A sex education class of fifth graders who are of many different religious backgrounds.
2. A group of Catholic priests and nuns.

Notice that you will need to use a very different voice when writing for a very different audience. Divide into groups who wrote for the same audience. Pick one draft to share as a representative of Group 1 and one for Group 2.

CHAPTER ▶SIX

The Environment: A Delicate Balance

▶Prewriting

How threatened is the environment in which we live? There are daily reports in the media about pollution, the disappearance of the ozone layer, and other hazards. Many of us who live in urban centers recycle wastes so that they will not become a part of the growing problem of hazardous refuse. Our children learn about saving the environment in elementary schools, and ecological science has taken its place in many high school curricula. Yet we are often confused about the extent to which our world is endangered.

EXERCISE 1: Thinking About the Issue

In groups or pairs discuss the answers to these questions.

1. What do you think should be done in your neighborhood to protect the environment?
2. How can the individual citizen of the planet make a contribution to keeping it safe for future generations?
3. What do you think government can do to improve the environment?
4. Rank the following in order of importance in terms of danger to the average citizen:
   - **a.** Pesticide residue on foods eaten by humans
   - **b.** Hazardous waste sites (in use)
   - **c.** The greenhouse warming effect
   - **d.** Radiation from nuclear power plant accidents
   - **e.** Hazardous waste sites (abandoned)
   - **f.** Radiation from x-rays
   - **g.** Industrial accidents releasing pollutants into the air, water, or soil
   - **h.** Exposure to toxic chemicals in the workplace
   - **i.** Destruction of protective ozone layer
   - **j.** Non-hazardous wastes, like trash disposal
   - **k.** Underground storage tanks leaking gasoline and other substances
   - **l.** Pesticides harming farmers, farm workers, and consumers who work with them.

▶Reading Selection

The preceding list of environmental hazards is taken from an article by William K. Stevens in *The New York Times*. The article examines the debate over the issues you have just considered. After you read the article, you will find a list of environmental risks that the experts have ranked in order of importance. Compare it with the list you ranked with your peers in the preceding exercise.

What Really Threatens the Environment?

By William K. Stevens

1 Are Americans preoccupied with relatively modest environmental threats while neglecting big ones that could unleash **catastrophe**?

2 To a large extent, some scientists and government officials believe, the answer is yes. William K. Reilly, the Administrator of the

Environmental Protection Agency, told a Senate committee in Washington on Friday that in many cases, the public and Congress are at odds with scientists over which environmental threats are the most serious. He has begun a campaign to reassess those priorities, and he leaves no doubt that his money is on the scientists.

3 "Sound science is our most reliable compass," he says in speeches calling for the nation to establish environmental priorities.

4 Mr. Reilly's campaign is intended to stimulate a national debate over environmental goals. And at a time when many of the most obvious and clear-cut environmental threats like air pollution and water pollution have been addressed and more subtle, complex problems are coming to the fore, the campaign may usher in a new, more complicated and more **contentious** phase in the national environmental struggle.

Mismatch of Perceptions

5 There seems little doubt of a mismatch between public perceptions of environmental risk and those of the scientists. Oil spills, hazardous waste, underground storage tanks and releases of radioactive materials, for instance, have aroused high emotions, generated reams of reports and prodded Congress to spend billions of dollars. Opinion surveys place them in the front ranks of public concern about the environment.

6 But in terms of the actual **magnitude** of risk they pose, scientists advising the E.P.A. rate them near the bottom of a broad **array** of environmental threats. This, the scientists say, is because their effects are relatively limited or **short-lived** or both.

7 At the same time, global warming and the destruction and alteration of natural habitats rank relatively low in public perception, polls show. But the scientists place them among the top risks because their potential consequences appear to be so damaging in the long run and their effects so widespread and difficult to reverse.

8 Federal environmental laws "are more reflective of public perceptions of risk than of scientific understanding of risk," the E.P.A. Science Advisory Board said in a report on environmental risks last fall. The scientists' report was the basis for Friday's hearings. Mr. Reilly and others say environmental problems are addressed unevenly, usually on the basis of **episodic**, momentary public anxieties about problems that, while frightening, represent a relatively limited threat: contamination of a local waterway by hazardous wastes, for example.

9 No one is suggesting that these problems should be ignored. Oil spills and other low-ranking risks can cause "real damage where and when they occur," Mr. Reilly told the senators. But, he said, "they are in a different league compared to some of our other problems, such as stratospheric ozone depletion[1] and climate change, which have the potential to affect life everywhere, and for many years to come."

10 The advisory board identified four environmental threats to health that it said were in the front rank: outdoor air pollution, exposure of workers to chemicals, indoor air pollution and pollutants in drinking water.

Major Environmental Threats

11 It established three categories of risk for threats that humans pose to the environment. Relatively high-risk problems of this nature included the global warming that many scientists predict will result from an increase in heat-trapping atmospheric gases produced by human activity; depletion of the ozone shield that protects Earth from the Sun's harmful ultraviolet radiation, and destruction and **alteration** of natural habitats and the extinction of species, with an accompanying loss of biological diversity.

12 A middle rank included **herbicides** and **pesticides**, pollution of surface waters, acid precipitation and airborne toxic substances. Relatively low risk was assigned to oil spills, escape of radioactive materials, **acid runoff** to surface waters and pollution of groundwater.

13 Risks in this area of ecological threats were assigned largely on the basis of how many people a problem affects, how wide a geographical area is involved, and how serious and long-lasting the harm might be, according to Dr. William Cooper, a zoologist and aquatic ecologist at Michigan State University who headed the board's panel on ecological risks.

14 On that basis, oil spills, for example, ranked low because their effects on coastal areas are relatively short-term and local. "The public doesn't perceive it that way," Dr. Cooper said, "but those ecosystems bounce back real fast."

15 By contrast, he said, the loss of natural habitats and the disappearance of species are top risks because they affect the economic welfare of future generations worldwide and because the loss is "virtually irreversible." Similarly, ozone depletion and global

[1]stratospheric ozone depletion: diminishment of the protective layer of ozone in the earth's atmosphere. (The ozone layer protects living things from the sun's harmful ultraviolet rays.)

warming were placed in the top rank because they are worldwide problems and because their effects are potentially catastrophic and reversible only over decades.

16 Given the substantial cost of environmental protection, Mr. Reilly argues, it is all the more important to set sensible priorities as the next phase of environmental protection begins. The E.P.A. estimates the United States will spend nearly 3 percent of its gross national product[2] on environmental protection by the end of this decade. The nation "can probably afford to spend 3 percent," Mr. Reilly said, "but we're not rich enough to spend it in the wrong places."

Doubts are Raised

17 While many environmentalists and politicians say it is a good idea to set priorities, doubts and possible points of dispute are cropping up.

18 Environmentalists who have devoted themselves to causes ranked low on the priority list are unlikely to stop pushing their interests. Others resist anything that might look like an effort to practice environmental **triage**, concentrating on some problems to the exclusion of others.

19 "I don't quarrel with the conclusion that global warming is the No.1 threat," said David Doniger, a senior lawyer with the Natural Resources Defense Council. "But I don't think the only way you can tackle global warming is by not tackling hazardous wastes. We can and should, and can afford to, do it all."

20 Several Senators questioned on Friday whether scientists knew enough to set priorities confidently. Senator Dave Durenberger, Republican of Minnesota, asked whether science was as good a guide as public values. People know what environmental assets are important to pass on to future generations, he said.

21 The Science Advisory Board acknowledged that assessing relative risks was an imprecise science, since much was unknown about some environmental threats. The board noted in its report that environmental policy-making "necessarily embodies subjective values" and that policy-makers should take both science and public perceptions into account.

22 As more complex and challenging environmental threats dominate the discussion, the debate will probably be complicated by increasing uncertainty about the nature of environmental risks, noted Senator Daniel Patrick Moynihan, the New York Democrat

[2]gross national product: the total value of goods and services produced in one year by the entire economy of a country.

who presided over the hearing. Science, he said, is a matter of complexity and probability, not simple certainty.

23 What this means is that when science is **invoked** as a guide to priorities, as Mr. Reilly and others believe it must be, clear-cut answers are harder to come by. As science investigates an issue, it often tends to raise as many questions as it answers. In the eyes of the public, this could weaken the claim of science as an arbiter[3] of priorities.

24 But on the biggest risks, some scientists argue, uncertainty must not become cause for inaction. Much is uncertain about the magnitude and effects of global warming, for instance. By the time scientists know whether they are right or wrong about predictions of climatic catastrophe, Dr. Cooper said, it will be too late to do anything.

25 This requires "a whole different **mindset**," Dr. Cooper said. "You don't care about being right," he said. "You just don't want to be wrong. Once the cost of being wrong gets too high, you go into a risk **aversion** mode. You avoid the risk no matter what the cost."

What's a Serious Hazard?

[Here are the hazards considered the most dangerous by the experts:]

Relatively High-Risk Ecological Problems:

Habitat alteration and destruction (soil erosion, deforestation, etc.)
Species extinction and overall loss of biological diversity
Stratospheric ozone depletion
Global climate change (greenhouse warming)

Relatively High Risks to Human Health:

Outdoor pollutants
Worker exposure to chemicals in industry and agriculture
Air pollution indoors
Pollutants in drinking water

Relatively Medium-Risk Ecological Problems:

Herbicides and pesticides
Pollution of surface water
Acid deposition (acid rain, etc.)
Airborne **toxic** substances

Relatively Low-Risk Ecological Problems:

Oil spills
Groundwater pollution (hazardous wastes, underground tanks, etc.)

---

[3]arbiter: one having the power to judge or decide.

Escape of radioactive materials
Acid runoff to surface waters
Thermal pollution

William K. Stevens, "What Really Threatens the Environment?" *The New York Times,* 29 January, 1991.

EXERCISE 2: Understanding the Reading

Divide into groups or pairs and write the answers to the following. You may decide as a group on the best answer to each and present it to the rest of the class.

1. In the article you just read, there are two points of view about threats which face the environment: that of the public and that of the experts. What are these two perspectives, and why do they exist?

2. What three categories of risk levels for environmental hazards have been established?

3. How much is the United States spending on environmental concerns, according to the E.P.A.?

4. What debates and disputes have arisen between scientists and politicians, and why?

5. What would be your environmental risk of highest concern if you were:

   a. a farmer?

   b. an astronaut?

   c. a pregnant woman?

   d. the president of a major oil-producing corporation?

   e. a worker at a plastics factory?

6. In the Prewriting section you were asked to rank the environmental concerns so that they would reflect those you considered most important. How does your list differ from that of the experts presented at the end of the reading selection?

EXERCISE 3: Vocabulary

acid runoff	contentious	invoked	short-lived
alteration	episodic	magnitude	thermal
array	groundwater	mindset	toxic
aversion	herbicides	pesticides	triage
catastrophe			

Use a dictionary to help you answer the following questions about word parts and word derivations.

1. Two of the vocabulary words from this article are similar: *herbicide* and *pesticide* share a suffix. Other words with that same suffix include *homicide*, *fratricide*, *matricide*, *patricide*, and *suicide*. Herbicides and pesticides are certain types of chemicals; the other five words refer to names of specific types of crimes. What meaning do these words, all ending with *-icide*, have in common?
2. *Thermal* is an adjective, used at the end of the article you just read, to modify the word "pollutant." The root, *therm-*, is a common one. It can be found in *thermometer*, *thermostat*, even in the brand name *Thermos*, which refers to products used to keep drinks and foods warm or cold. *Therm-* comes from a Greek word. What does that Greek word mean?
3. Doctors use the word *triage* to refer to the grim process of deciding among many patients who should be treated first, and sometimes who should be treated and who should not. (Triage is most often an issue in emergency combat hospitals and other disaster scenes.) The author of the article you just read adapted the concept of triage in paragraph 18. What does it mean in this context?
4. There are several compound words in this list: *short-lived* (paragraph 6), *acid runoff* (list at the end of the article), *mindset* (paragraph 25), and *groundwater* (list at the end of the article). The components of each of these words are themselves short, simple words. Without looking them up, figure out what these compounds mean. Then go back and check the context of each one so that you understand its use in context.
5. In Latin, the word *magnus* means great or large. A *magnate* is a powerful or influential person. To make something tiny look larger, you would use a *magnifying glass*. An artist's greatest work, her lifetime achievement, might be called her *magnum opus*. Which of the listed vocabulary words is related to all these words? What does it mean? Name another English word that is derived from the same root.
6. See if you can determine the meanings of each highlighted word in the Stevens article from the context in which it appears. Then check the meaning in the Glossary in the back of this book.

You will know you have learned the word when you can recognize it in another context, and when you can use it easily when you speak or write.

▶Writing the Draft

TOPIC: Concern about the environment has become a major issue of the '90s. Write a draft of a letter to Mr. William K. Reilly, the Administrator of the Environmental Protection Agency. In it, state your opinion as to what should be done about the problems of the environment. Use specifics, including facts from the article you just read to support your point.

▶Revising

Compare the draft you wrote with the two student drafts that follow.

Student Draft 1

1 Dear Mr. Reilly,
The environment is an increasingly important issue in our world today. Most of us do not think about this issue in our daily lives. We are too busy just getting from day to day, trying to make a living and raise our children.

2 But children are the future, and if we do care about them, what kind of planet will they live in to old age and raise their children in? We know that there is a real danger from the sun's toxic rays that cause cancer with the depletion of the ozone layer, for instance. We also know that the use of automobiles contributes to this hazard, yet most people continue to buy and use their own automobiles instead of using public transportation.

3 Why do we do this? We do it because we are too selfish and too short-sighted to care about any long-term damage to the ozone layer and the planet Earth.

4 In my opinion, the lawmakers of this country should pass laws forcing people who can do it to use public transportation a certain percentage of the time. I realize that this sounds drastic, but we must take serious steps to avoid disaster.

Student Draft 2

1 Dear Mr. Reilly:
I am writing this letter to you in the name of all the citizens who live in a large city. The purpose of this letter is to find a solution

to many problems that we are facing in our society. My complaints are because the government is not doing enough to regulate the pollution. There are many contaminants in this city affecting the citizens.

2 The most important things that cause pollution are garbage, cars, and chemical products. Some of the chemical products cause a lot of sicknesses, especially in pregnant women. The women breathe the toxics that are caused by chemical products of factories. Sometimes when the women give birth, the babies are born with problems. I believe that the government should find another way to manufacture those products without affecting our citizen's health.

3 Here in my neighborhood, people are directly affected because of the local government deciding to burn all the garbage and recyclable wastes here in a nearby dumping area. The neighbors where I live are complaining because burning the garbage is affecting their health, especially that of women and children. I think that legislation should be passed at both the local and federal levels forcing the city to look for an empty and faraway place to burn garbage where it will not affect the citizens here.

4 Please help us resolve the problem in this country's cities of burning garbage and toxic wastes. Our cities should be kept clean and a healthy environment so that visitors will want to stay and help its economy. Current environmental policy is hurting the health and economy of our city.

Are these drafts convincing? Which one is more effective? Why? What advice would you give to the writers in order to revise their letters into more convincing arguments?

▶WRITING FOCUS: Using Authoritative Evidence

One of the ways in which a writer can convince the reader that the opinion in his essay is valid is to use evidence from authorities. An authority is an information source (a person, an organization, a textbook, etc.). The more likely it is that the reader will automatically respect your source and accept its knowledge and honesty on a subject, the more authoritative that source is.

EXERCISE 4: Authoritative Sources

Read the fictional sentences below. In each of the examples, tell whether you would be *very likely* or *very unlikely* to accept without question the source presented as authoritative on the subject matter at issue.

1. Ex-President Bush said that the AIDS virus was not transferable through casual contact.
2. Ex-President Bush said that the Republican Party was in a better position than at any time in this century.
3. Jacques Cousteau told the audience that the problems of global warming and overpopulation would have a greater effect on the next generation than the oil fires in Kuwait and the wreck of the *Exxon Valdez*.
4. My English professor said that my writing had improved since the beginning of the semester.
5. My English professor believes the destruction of the rain forests in Brazil will bring an end to life on this planet in 30 years.
6. The President of the Sierra Club wrote an article in which she said that college students today don't care at all about the environment.

Citing an authoritative source can be a powerful tool in argumentation if it is done correctly. Clearly, as you can see from Exercise 4, you must match the authority with the appropriate subject matter. Above all, be clear about what your point is, because although you may use other writers to back up your own ideas, the most important writer of your composition is *you*.

EXERCISE 5: A Checklist for Using Authoritative Evidence

1. Look at the article from *The New York Times* by Stevens. What authorities does Stevens cite on environmental concerns? Do you feel these are highly authoritative sources?
2. Here are some questions to ask when using authoritative evidence:
   - **a.** Is the authority appropriate as a spokesperson on this topic?
   - **b.** Is the authority prejudiced in the presentation of his or her point of view and supporting evidence?
   - **c.** Is the authority up to date in his or her work on the topic?

d. Can the evidence from this authority be useful in presenting the argument?

3. Examine the use of authoritative evidence in your own draft and the student drafts in this chapter.

EXERCISE 6: Using the Library to Find Authoritative Evidence

1. Go to the reference section of a library and find some evidence to support some of the issues presented in the article on the environment by Stevens.

2. Find an authority which offers a completely different point of view from the ones discussed so far in this chapter.

3. Has your opinion on your topic changed? If so, revise your draft accordingly.

4. Can you use any of this additional information in your argument?

5. Remember, if you use evidence from another source, you *must* include the name and all the information of that source in your writing to avoid plagiarism. In order to use correct form, consult the *MLA* or *APA Style Manual.*

▶Revising

EXERCISE 7: Revising Questions

Revise your draft. Here are the questions we have been using as a checklist for revising in each chapter. You may know them by heart by now.

1. Is the writer's main idea (his or her "point") stated clearly in the first paragraph?

2. Does each idea and each paragraph follow logically from one to the next? How does each idea *relate* to the one that precedes and follows it?

3. Are all ideas related specifically to the opinion being put forth in this draft? If not, which ones could be eliminated?

4. Which sentences explain, illustrate, or give examples about the topic?

5. What is the main idea of each paragraph? Is the idea adequately explained and developed?

6. Which ideas are particularly interesting? Could the writer add more details to develop this part of the draft? (Could information from the Stevens article be used?)

7. Could a personal anecdote be added to make the argument more convincing? (Use the question words, *Who? What? Where? When? Why? How?* to help you develop your example with specific words.)
8. Does the conclusion seem to provide an adequate ending to the discussion of the topic?
9. Can you think of any questions that you could ask the writer that would help in the revision process?
10. Read the draft backwards (from the last paragraph to the first). Do you still feel that each paragraph is connected to the one preceding it?

▶ SCREENING ROOM

Captain Kirk, Mr. Spock, and the rest of the intrepid crew of the *Starship Enterprise* have to leave their own 25th century, and journey through time to 1980s California in order to obtain a mating pair of humpback whales, in *Star Trek IV: The Voyage Home*. It seems that sometime between our era and theirs, the humpbacks became extinct; a crisis in the 25th century is precipitated when an apocalyptic message from deep space is mysteriously broadcast in a language that can only be understood by the great sea mammals which haven't been seen in hundreds of years. *Star Trek IV* (which is available at most video stores) delivers, in a somewhat humorous (and highly entertaining) form, the message about the importance of species survival, and that extinct is forever—unless you believe we'll be able to travel backwards through time.

EXERCISE 8: Thinking About the Movie

1. What are some of the changes in everyday life the movie presumes will take place over the next 400 years?
2. Why is species survival important?

▶Editing: Articles

The common English words *the*, *a*, and *an* are called *articles*. An article is a type of modifier, a kind of adjective that precedes a noun and modifies it.

Articles can present a problem for many writers whose native language is not English. This is often because the use of articles differs in the native language. For example, a Spanish speaker will say *la vida* for *life* in English.

Here are a few general rules that will help you.

1. Use *a* to specify a particular place or thing that is mentioned for the first time. [*Note: An* is the same as *a*, but is used when the word that follows begins with a vowel or a vowel sound.]

   A man got into *an* automobile.

2. Use *the* when there is a specific thing referred to that has been mentioned previously.

   The man who got into *the* automobile was arrested.

3. However, there are many situations that are considered specific:
   - **a.** something that is unique for everyone in the world, for example:

     the sun, *the* moon, *the* stars

   - **b.** something made specific by its setting, for example:

     He put *the* windows up in *the* car.

   - **c.** someone or something known by a specific group, for example:

     The president made his opinion on peace clear.

   - **d.** anything or anyone the writer specifies by the context in which it, he, or she appears.

     He went to meet with *the* professor who teaches *the* course.

4. Omit articles before proper nouns as names of persons, streets, cities, continents, countries, lakes, and mountains, for example:
   He lives on Fifth Avenue. (not *the* Fifth Avenue)

   However, *the* may be used with plural proper nouns, for example:

   The Mayan ruins are found deep in *the* jungles of Guatemala.

5. Omit articles before mass nouns or nouns that refer to things in a general sense, for example:

Jean stored sugar and tea in her kitchen. (not *the* sugar and *the* tea)

6. Sometimes articles are used to determine generic meaning. (Generic can mean a kind or class of things, rather than an individual one.) For example:

A teacher is *a* person who helps *an* individual realize his or her potential in *a* career area.

This last category is difficult. You may need to check with your instructor or a grammar book when you have questions.

EXERCISE 9: Checking Articles

Find the mistakes in this student essay.

New evidence about acid rain suggests that the many beautiful pyramids in the Mexico are being destroyed by this form of chemicals carried by rain. The ancient Mayan civilizations have left us legacy of pyramids and the colorful murals. As more and more ruins are discovered, we are able to understand how the ancient civilization indigenous to this continent lived. Black crusts are forming over temples at the Palenque, Chichen-Itza, and the Uzmal.

And the most important of all for scientists, the Mayan writing on the ancient buildings is being obscured, so that an epigraphers will have the difficulty translating them. As for the dangerous effect that pollution is having on environment, this evidence is presenting a strong case that pollution is even more intense of a problem than once thought. If the polluted air is having this destructive effect on the surface of stone stelae, what is it doing to person's body?

After you have finished revising and editing, hand in your composition and the drafts for evaluation.

▶Writing with Time, Topic, and Audience Constraints

EXERCISE 10: Writing a Timed Essay

Jacques Cousteau and his family have been known for decades as advocates for the marine environment. Pioneers in the science of marine biology, they have enlightened the world as to the importance of the ocean's role in maintaining a healthy planet. Cousteau's concerns as presented in his publication *Calypso Log* have also focused on the fact that overpopulation of the earth will contribute to its destruction by promoting massive problems of pollution from overcrowding, not to mention the hardship on children born to poverty and neglect.

Write an essay in one hour on the following topic:

Population control will help promote a healthier world by reducing pollution, poverty, and overcrowding.

Write your opinion, giving specific reasons why you hold your viewpoint. When you finish, read your composition aloud to your partner or group members. How does your composition differ from those of the rest of the group? What did you learn from the feedback you just received?

CHAPTER
▸SEVEN

Sticks, Stones, and Words: Freedom of Speech

▸Prewriting

Throughout history, many among the waves of immigrants who have come to the United States have done so because of terrible economic and political conditions in their native countries. Although the "promised land" of America is often exaggerated, many of these people found certain freedoms available in the U.S. that were not available back home.

EXERCISE 1: Defining the Term

1. What is *freedom of speech*? In your own words, write a definition.
2. Does freedom of speech exist in your native country? Explain.

3. Does freedom of speech exist in the United States?
4. Is there any context in which you are not free to express any ideas you wish, in any form you wish?
5. Are there any disadvantages in having freedom of expression? Explain.

EXERCISE 2: Thinking About the Issue

1. In one paragraph, express in your own words the meaning of the First Amendment.
2. Explain in your own words at least one reason that the freedoms guaranteed in the First Amendment are significant.

▶Reading Selections

A notable—and sometimes controversial—freedom guaranteed by the Constitution of the United States is the freedom of speech, that is, the right to say, write, or otherwise express oneself without restriction by law. This is part of the message of the First Amendment to the Constitution. Here is what that amendment, at the beginning of the Bill of Rights, states, exactly as it was written by the Constitution's authors and approved by the states in 1789.

> Congress shall make no law respecting an establishment of religion, or prohibiting the free exercise thereof;[1] or abridging[2] the freedom of speech, or of the press; or of the right of the people peaceably to assemble, and to petition the Government for a redress[3] of **grievances**.

In 1991, a student at Brown University in Providence, Rhode Island, was expelled from the school after an incident in which he drunkenly shouted offensive remarks at fellow students on campus. The incident, and the university's reaction to it, raised a number of interesting issues related to freedom of expression.

Excerpted below are, first, an article about the incident; an editorial; and several letters to the editor, including one from Vartan Gregorian, the Brown president who upheld the decision to expel the student.

All of these are taken from *The New York Times*.

---

[1]thereof: of that.
[2]abridging: reducing.
[3]redress: make right.

STUDENT AT BROWN IS EXPELLED UNDER A RULE BARRING "HATE SPEECH"

1 Brown University has expelled a student for shouting racial epithets, thereby violating an anti-harassment rule enacted in 1989 as part of an effort by the university to combat racism on campus. It is the first time a Brown student has been expelled for such a violation and is thought to be the first such expulsion in the country....

2 The student, Douglas Hann, a junior, was found by the university's Undergraduate Disciplinary Council to have violated the rule by shouting anti-black, anti-Semitic, and anti-homosexual remarks in a courtyard last October. The council, made up of five students and five faculty or administration members, also considered that he had been drinking at the time and that it was his second violation involving racial epithets....

3 A witness...said Mr. Hann was yelling an anti-black comment involving a common obscenity and the word "nigger," in the courtyard of a dormitory. He said the remark was yelled into the air and did not appear to be directed at any individual.

4 A student in the dormitory then opened his window and shouted "Keep it down," the witness said. Mr. Hann then used the word "faggot" and an obscenity combined with the word "Jew," directing his shouts at the student in the window.

5 Mr. Hann does not deny the incident but says the allegations as presented in university hearings were inexact. He declined to specify exactly what he had said, either during the incident or during his hearings.

6 In the telephone interview, Mr. Hann said Mr. Gregorian "wanted someone," adding, "I think it was just a political statement by the university."...

7 The case was the second charge against Mr. Hann that led to university hearings. In his first year at Brown, a committee of students and faculty members found Mr. Hann guilty of directing a racial epithet at a black student in a fraternity bar on Jan. 27, 1989. His punishment then was to attend a race relations workshop and counseling for possible alcohol abuse.

8 In April 1989, just 20 days after his inauguration as president, Mr. Gregorian addressed a group of students after racist graffiti and white supremacist leaflets were found in a dormitory.

9 "I issue a solemn warning that it is the policy of my administration to take action against those who incite hatred," Mr. Gregorian said. "It is my intention to prosecute vigorously, and to expel immediately, such individual or individuals for any attempt

to inject and promote racism and thus insult the dignity of our students as citizens of Brown."...

The New York Times, February 12, 1991

Editorial:
HOW MUCH HATE TO TOLERATE

1 Free speech and human relations seemed to collide last month at Brown University when it expelled a student for racial and religious harassment. In fact, however, to judge by all that is publicly known, the school walked a fine line with sensitivity toward its complex mission.

2 One mission of a university is to send into the world graduates who are tolerant of many races, faiths and cultures. Another mission is to teach the value of free expression and tolerance even for hateful ideas. But should such tolerance cover racist, sexist or homophobic speech that makes the learning environment intolerable for racial and religious minorities, women and other targets of abuse? Brown found a reasonable basis for saying, clearly, no....

3 If the facts are reported correctly, Mr. Hann crossed the line between merely hateful speech and hateful speech that directly confronted and insulted other undergraduates.

4 Some courts have found that public universities are bound by the First Amendment's ban on state censorship and thus may not punish students for expressing politically incorrect or socially distasteful ideas. Brown, like other private schools, is less directly bound by the Constitution but committed to its **precepts**. It is trying to avoid censorship but draws a line between strong language and what the courts often call "fighting words."...

5 The lines may not be so clearly drawn in other cases. There may also be more of them in the present climate of evidently increasing student intolerance. But when **bigots** attack other students with ugly **invective**, universities, whether public or private, need not remain silent. Their presidents, like Mr. Gregorian, may denounce indecency and, in so doing, protect tolerance.

The New York Times, February 21, 1991

Letter to the editor:
BROWN EXPULSION NOT ABOUT FREE SPEECH

1 [Your article {see pages 111–112}] suggests I have instituted "hate-speech" prohibitions at Brown University.... Brown University has never expelled anyone for free speech, nor will it ever do so....

2 The university's code of conduct [which has been read and agreed to in writing by all entering students] does not prohibit speech; it prohibits actions, and these include behavior that "shows **flagrant** disrespect for the well-being of others or is unreasonably disruptive of the university community."

3 [It] prohibits inappropriate, abusive, threatening or demeaning actions based on race, religion, gender, handicap, ethnicity, national origin or sexual orientation....

4 The rules do not proscribe[1] words, epithets[2] or **slanders**; they proscribe behavior. The point at which speech becomes behavior and the degree to which that behavior shows flagrant disrespect for the well-being of others,... subjects someone to abusive or demeaning actions... or is related to drug or alcohol use is determined by a hearing to consider the circumstances of each case. The student is entitled to an appeal, which includes review by a senior officer and a decision by the president....

5 Freedom-of-speech questions lie at the heart of any academic community. The very nature of the academic enterprise necessitates that universities remain partisans of heterodoxy,[3] of a rich and full range of opinions, ideas and expression. Imposed orthodoxies[4] of all sorts, including what is called "politically correct" speech, are **anathema** to our enterprise.

6 The university's most compelling challenge is to achieve a balance between the right of its individual members to operate and speak freely, and fostering respect for and adherence to community values and standards of conduct.

Vartan Gregorian
President, Brown University

The New York Times, February 21, 1991

More opinions about the topic:

The following three letters to the editor of *The New York Times* were published on March 16, 1991. They were grouped together under the headline:

---

[1]proscribe: limit.
[2]epithet: A term or name, often of an abusive nature, used to describe a person.
[3]heterodoxy: a belief that differs from accepted doctrine.
[4]orthodoxy: a belief that is traditional or commonly accepted.

BROWN BLURS LINE BETWEEN SPEECH AND ACTION

Letter 1

1 To the Editor:

"How Much Hate to Tolerate" (editorial, Feb. 21) endorses the position taken by Vartan Gregorian, president of Brown University, who purports to explain in "Brown Expulsion Not About Free Speech," a letter on the same page, the expulsion of Douglas Hann, a student, for shouting racial and homophobic epithets on campus. Mr. Gregorian maintains that speech becomes behavior when it "shows flagrant disrespect for the well-being of others." This is pure sophistry.

2 All speech is conduct. It is protected conduct because it is a form of expression that encompasses the capacity to communicate ideas.

3 The line separating speech and action serves as the most **practicably** defensible barrier to censorship. It is a line that the *Times* itself has repeatedly fortified when reporting has been alleged to disrespect the well-being of United States foreign policy, as in the case of the publication of the Pentagon Papers, or when reporting has been alleged to abuse or demean people in the news who have sued for **libel**.

4 Effective speech is seldom neutral. As Justice Oliver Wendell Holmes once observed, "every idea is an incitement." However, an incitement to hatred is every bit as much a pretext to ban *Mein Kampf* as it is to oust a student from college because he brays like an ass.

5 The other side of the line separating speech and action is precipitating harm to others. As disgusting and disgraceful as the student's remarks were, unless the circumstances under which he shouted them constituted a clear and present danger to his fellow students, his punishment represents a miscarriage of justice, in that it violates both the letter and the spirit of the First Amendment.

6 Moreover, what lesson has this action taken by Brown taught Mr. Hann and his schoolmates: that authority defines liberty?

7 Far better, it seems to me, to exact from Mr. Hann a graduation requirement that he devote 50 hours of public service on behalf of AIDS patients (action) and then demonstrate that he has cleaned up his act as well by writing an essay explaining why what he did was wrong (speech), than to concede at this early stage in his development that he is incapable of learning.

Harvard Hollenberg

New York, Feb 27, 1991.

Letter 2

1 Hate that advocates bodily or psychological harm on another human being because of differences cannot be tolerated. Nor do I believe it is protected by the First Amendment....

2 ... Hate denies justice for the victim.

Hyman H. Haves

Letter 3

1 In endorsing Brown University's expulsion of a drunken student for shouting religious, homophobic and racial epithets at other students, your Feb. 21 editorial and letter from Vartan Gregorian... ignore First Amendment precepts.

2 The editorial and letter wrongly assume that "speech that makes the learning environment intolerable for racial and religious minorities, women and other targets of abuse" can somehow be surgically **excised** from academic discourse without damaging the vigorous, free debates that Mr. Gregorian calls "the heart of any academic community."

3 Both contend that Brown may expel students for speech or expressive conduct "that flagrantly disregards the well-being of others" or is "inappropriate, abusive, threatening or demeaning... based on race, religion, gender, handicap, ethnicity, nationality or sexual orientation."

4 These standards are so vague, and therefore subject to widespread discretionary enforcement, that students cannot know whether any particular speech is punishable unless or until university officials tell them so. Vesting[1] college officials with this power will inevitably chill campus debate. For these reasons, a similar code at the University of Michigan was recently ruled unconstitutional by a Federal court.

5 To be sure, the line between offensive speech, which is constitutionally protected, and offensive conduct, which is not, is often hard to draw. The guidelines of Brown, however, make no meaningful attempt to draw that line. Their overbroad reach was illustrated by their enforcement against a Brown student, Douglas Hann. Brown had no evidence that Mr. Hann engaged in harassment as we commonly understand it—the singling out of a particular individual for repeated intimidation. His isolated drunken outbursts can hardly be deemed such clear instances of proscribable harassment as to warrant the university's ultimate sanction.

---

[1]vesting: investing with authority or power; to assign authority to someone.

6 We agree that Mr. Gregorian may "denounce racist expressions." Indeed, he should do so. He has taken a dangerous further step, however. His action runs counter to the purpose of the Bill of Rights: to protect individual freedom from the tyranny of majority preferences. By subjecting Mr. Hann to its most extreme punishment, Brown risks making him a martyr.

Nadine Strosser
President
American Civil Liberties Union

EXERCISE 3: Thinking About the Issue from Different Points of View

1. Write in one paragraph how Douglas Hann might describe the incident which got him expelled from Brown.
2. Write in one paragraph how Brown president Vartan Gregorian would describe the incident, and why he expelled Mr. Hann.
3. Imagine you are a parent who is spending more than $40,000 for a Brown University education for your child. Write in one paragraph how you would describe the incident.
4. In one sentence, summarize each of the following:
   - the letter by A.C.L.U. President Nadine Strosser
   - the letter by Hyman H. Haves
   - the letter by Harvard Hollenberg

   How do these letters differ in their points of view?

EXERCISE 4: Vocabulary

anathema	grievances	precepts
bigots	invective	slanders
excised	libel	
flagrant	practicably	

Find each of the ten vocabulary words listed above in their context in the readings. (*Grievances* is in the First Amendment; the other nine are in *The New York Times* articles about the Douglas Hann incident.) See if you can figure out their meanings from the context. Then, check the meanings you deduced from the context in the Glossary. Finally, write a 1- to 3-paragraph summary of the Douglas Hann incident, in which you *use at least eight of the ten words.*

▶Writing the Draft

Write an essay in which you argue one side or the other of the question: should Douglas Hann have been expelled from the University? Or, should the University find some other reaction to Hann's behavior, because it is an example of free (even though offensive) speech?

▶WRITING FOCUS: Analogy

A tool often used in persuasive writing is *analogy*. We create an analogy when we say that one situation is like another situation. Then we use the similarity to help the reader understand our conclusion. For example:

Our family is like a monarchy: my parents are the king and queen, and my brothers and sisters and I are the subjects. Oh, sure, they listen to our input and they consider our desires, but in the end, it's their word that is law. They decide what's best for us.

As in any monarchy, the subjects only have a few choices. They can rebel, they can leave, or they can obey. Well, none of us is going to overthrow our parents. After all, like loyal subjects, we do love them. Mainly we obey. But as we grow up, sooner or later, each subject will leave the kingdom to set up his or her own monarchy.

This analogy works, in general terms, to describe the way authority is controlled in the writer's family, and the attitude each member has toward that authority. Consider this next analogy.

Racial hatred and bigotry is a cancer. Like any other cancer, it will grow until it kills the body in which it resides if it is not stopped and removed at an early stage.

For education to flourish, an atmosphere is needed that is tolerant, encouraging, creative, and open. Fear, intimidation, threats, and violence do not fit.

Brown University is the patient. Douglas Hann is the tumor. The only choice is surgery. We can only hope that the cancer hasn't spread.

Is this analogy, while powerful at first glance, completely acceptable? We may agree with the conclusion, but the analogy itself is not enough to support it, because unlike an actual cancer, there may be other ways of dealing with a bigoted student and a campus that is experiencing the presence of racism and intolerance.

Analogy works best when it is not leaned on too heavily. Can you think of an analogy that would work better in this case? Or, can you think of a way to use this analogy in some way, without drawing conclusions directly from it?

▶Revising

Read the following student draft.

Student Draft

1 Freedom is important in any society, but it has its limits. When you act in a way that is hurtful to another person, freedom is being carried too far. The student at Brown did not care whose feelings were hurt by the racist behavior. Thus, I think that it is important that there be some leadership, especially in an institution where learning is the focus. People in an education institution should learn how to behave, as well as learn subject matter.

2 The leadership that I am thinking of is that of the President. He was right in denouncing the behavior. He is setting the moral tone for the university. I do not think it necessary to expel the student, for that would be an infringement on democratic rights. But, just as we are not free to bodily harm someone, we should not be allowed to do so with words, even in a democracy. To do so should bring negative consequences upon the perpetrator. The student should be suspended for a period of time. This way, he would be forced to consider the seriousness of his act of disrespect.

3 Recently, there was an incident in an urban university in which a professor made racist comments. Just as with the student at Brown, there was much controversy as to what should be done in order to stop this behavior that was so injurious to the victim and to the university's reputation. The president denounced the comments, but the professor was not fired. Yet this professor, instead of being a role model, offended many people. In this case, perhaps the professor should be forced to take a leave of absence

without pay. If the inappropriate behavior continued, he should be terminated.

4 We are entering an era of moral decay. We should try to recognize that the above actions did not take place in a vacuum, but in an atmosphere of corrupt values and loss of integrity. We should examine our lives to see if each of us could live by more ethically sound principles, respecting ourselves and our colleagues and fellow inhabitants of the planet.

EXERCISE 5: Revising Questions

Divide into groups. One person in each group will read the preceding sample draft to his or her group. The following questions will help you rethink the composition for organization, coherence (the smooth interconnection of ideas), and development of supporting points. When you have finished applying these questions to the sample essay, use them on your own draft.

1. Is the writer's main idea (his or her "point") stated clearly in the first paragraph?
2. Does each idea and each paragraph follow logically from one to the next? How does each idea *relate* to the one that precedes and follows it?
3. Are all ideas related specifically to the opinion being put forth in this draft? If not, which ones could be eliminated?
4. Which sentences explain, illustrate, or give examples about the topic?
5. What is the main idea of each paragraph? Is the idea adequately explained and developed?
6. Which ideas are particularly interesting? Could the writer add more details to develop this part of the draft? (Could the writer have used details from *The New York Times* article, or one of the letters to the editor, about the incident at Brown? Where should these details be included?)
7. Could a personal anecdote be added to make the argument more convincing? (Use the question words, *Who? What? Where? When? Why? How?* to help you develop your example with specific words.)
8. Does the conclusion seem to provide an adequate ending to the discussion of the topic?
9. Can you think of any questions that you could ask the writer that would help in the revision process?

10. Read the draft backwards (from the last paragraph to the first). Do you still feel that each paragraph is connected to the one preceding it?

▶ **SCREENING ROOM**

An important and interesting First Amendment issue lies at the heart of the plot of *Absence of Malice*, a fine 1981 film starring Paul Newman and Sally Field. Written by a former reporter, it tells of a conflict between a newspaper reporter's freedom of expression and an innocent man's damaged reputation. It is widely available at video stores.

EXERCISE 6: Thinking About the Movie

1. Write a synopsis or summary of the movie.
2. How could this story be used to illustrate an argument for or against freedom of expression?

▶Editing: Run-on Sentences

Run-on sentences are a very common writing problem. One practice that leads to run-ons is an incorrect use of the comma, known as a *comma splice*. This is the inappropriate joining of two sentences with a comma. In most of these cases, there are two excellent alternatives: either (1) use a period, and simply make two separate sentences; or (2) use the comma with an appropriate conjunction to make a correct compound sentence.

Look at the example below of a run-on sentence with an incorrect comma splice. Then read the two successful solutions to the problem.

Wrong:

The U.S Constitution would not be such a brilliant document without the First Amendment, freedom of speech is essential in a thriving democracy.

Right:

The U.S Constitution would not be such a brilliant document without the First Amendment. Freedom of speech is essential in a thriving democracy.

Right:

The U.S Constitution would not be such a brilliant document without the First Amendment, because freedom of speech is essential in a thriving democracy.

In the first correction, the run-on was made into two sentences. In the second correction, the run-on was made into an acceptable sentence by the addition of *because*.

EXERCISE 7: Comma Splices

Rewrite the paragraph below, correcting all the run-on sentences by eliminating bad comma splices. Try to use both of the means of correcting this problem that you learned from the example you just read.

Freedom of expression is a nice idea in general, I don't like the way some people use it. There's too much rude, offensive talk on the radio, too much sex on TV, don't they know children could be listening or watching, even late at night? When our country is at war reporters try to give so much information, our own men could be jeopardized, the enemy reads our newspapers too, you know. Let's have freedom of expression when it doesn't hurt anyone or put anyone at risk, that makes more sense than letting everybody shoot their mouths off whenever they want to. If you agree with me, use your freedom of expression to tell your Congressmen what to do, they just might listen.

▶Writing with Time, Topic, and Audience Constraints

EXERCISE 8: Writing a Timed Essay

The following scenario is fictional. Unfortunately, however, it is not unlike certain actual incidents that have taken place in recent semesters on American college campuses.

At a major East Coast university, a group of white students from Alabama have stirred up some unrest by hanging a Confederate Flag[1] in

---

[1]The Confederate Flag, which is the same as the state flag of Alabama, was also the national flag of the Confederate States of America during the American Civil War. Both northerners and southerners consider it a symbol of the "Old South."

the window of their dormitory. Some black students and some others find it to be offensive, but the Alabamians have thus far refused to take it down, citing their First Amendment rights to freedom of expression. There have followed public protests, and also anonymous threats. The problem escalated when first the dorm with the flag was vandalized, and then a burning cross was placed on the lawn of a fraternity house in which many of the members are black.

In neither case have the perpetrators of these incidents yet been caught. Naturally, the two sides accuse one another while proclaiming their own innocence, saying that the crimes were committed by parties trying to make someone "look bad." Meanwhile, the Dean of Students has agreed that the flag is an act of self-expression, and as such can not be repressed. She asked the boys to voluntarily remove it, but they have not.

Finally the situation has come to a head. A student who is black, claiming her own right of self-expression, has hung a Nazi flag from the window of her room. More protests and counter protests are taking place every day, as the entire campus is becoming polarized. It seems like everyone is angry at everyone else, and the only thing everyone seems to agree on is that there is going to be trouble if something doesn't change soon.

You are the editor of the daily student newspaper. Almost every student on campus reads your newspaper. Leaders of several different student groups, as well as a delegation of faculty members and the Dean of the university have all contacted you; they are all convinced that the only thing that can avert a crisis is an editorial written by someone whom *all* the students trust: YOU.

Your deadline is in two hours. Your topic is clear. Your audience: every student on campus. You had better make your point.

APPENDICES

►Appendix 1: Editing Exercises

The following exercises are designed to give help to those who need additional practice with editing their final copy for English grammar errors. They are to be used to supplement the exercises that already exist as part of each chapter, in the Editing section.

Each exercise will include a summary of the rules governing each grammar structure. For a more complete explanation, consult a grammar text, such as *A Grammar of Contemporary English* by Quirk, Greenbaum and Svartvik (Longman:1972, Heinle & Heinle).

I. Articles

A. The correct use of *the* and *a/an* can be difficult for students of other linguistic backgrounds to learn. Here are some basic rules.

- Articles go before nouns to modify or slightly change their meanings. The words *a/an* and *the* are used in this category.
- *The* is used to determine, in the following, definiteness or indefiniteness. (Definite nouns require the definite article.) *The* can be either singular or plural.

  The sun and *the* moon exist in our universe.

  There is only one sun, and one moon; therefore, the writer of this sentence is referring to one specific, definite item.

  The students chipped in to buy Dr. Watkins-Goffman's Christmas gift.

  The writer is referring to a *specific group* of students.

- When a group or class of people or things is being referred to *generally*, no article is required.

  Teachers usually receive a pension at retirement.

  In this sentence, *teachers* refers to a group of people in general; therefore, it does not need an article.

- The indefinite article *a* (or *an* when it immediately precedes a vowel sound) is used for group or generic meaning. *A* denotes singularity, oneness. (In fact, you can substitute the word *one* for the word *a* or *an* in a sentence without changing the meaning.)

  A person should never drink and drive.

- Indefinite nouns in the plural do not require any article.

  New people came into the factory.

- The first time a noun is introduced, it usually takes an indefinite article *(a)*. Second and all subsequent references to that same individual take the definite article *(the)*.

  A bank robber was running down Fifteenth Street, pursued by *a* police officer. *The* robber tried to resist, but *the* police officer quickly handcuffed *the* man.

  By the time you get to the second sentence, the reader knows which robber is being referred to.

- In English, a proper noun does not require an article, unless it is plural.

  Paris is my favorite city.

  The singular proper noun *Paris* needs no article.

  The New York Mets signed autographs for the young fans.

- The following are nouns that refer to fields of study. They usually do not require an article.

  chemistry

  physics

  mathematics

  Physics is more difficult than chemistry.

- In addition, articles are not used with the following:

- most ailments

  Shakti has *arthritis*.

- names of most holidays

  They had a family celebration for *Thanksgiving*.

- names of magazines and places in the neighborhood

  He read *Life* magazine when he went to *school*.

- nouns that denote abstract concepts such as:

  life

  freedom

  justice

The best kind of *life* includes *freedom* of speech and *justice*.

There are many rules governing the use of articles. Consult a grammar book if you have further questions.

B. Carefully read the following student essay, paying particular attention to the use of articles.

1 The university education is one of the biggest and most important goals in the life, and at the same time, one of the more distant. The medicine is the interest that I plan to study for the career. The high cost of the life and an everyday stress of the living is making that education an unrealistic dream.

2 Every day a prices for everything in this country are rising more and more, and this makes the people want to forget dream of university education. It stops being their most important goal in the life. Money that would be buying the books would be whole day's wages in factory. People at the present time have to work the double time that they had worked before to earn same money. Because of this economic problem, even more difficult social problem is created. Everyday people must work harder to pay the rent, buy food, pay expenses of raising children. For example, many women are like my friend Leela. She has a baby boy, Rahul. She has to take care of the Rahul because she can not afford to pay baby sitter. The Leela has to wait to resume her study after a Rahul has started the school.

3 In conclusion, because of the economic inflation, I cannot study the statistics and the biology for my career goal. I have wanted to be

doctor for long time. Now I have to think of another way to contribute to the mankind.

Circle the articles in the student essay that have been used incorrectly. Add an article wherever you think one is needed.

C. Now look at your own draft that you are revising. Correct any similar errors.

II. Subject-Verb Agreement

A. We discussed the rules for subject-verb agreement in the simple present tense in Chapter 4. For a summary, review the following:

- A present tense verb describes action that takes place in the present. It is also used to describe action that takes place repeatedly. Following is a model of how the present tense is used with regular verbs:

singular	**plural**
I think	we think
you think	you (plural) think
he thinks	they think
she thinks	
it thinks	

As you can see, in the third person (he, she, it), the verb has an -*s* ending. This is true for all regular verbs. (The determining factor is the identification of the subject. If the subject is third person singular, add -*s* to the verb.)

The *children*, whenever they are with their father, *watch* television.

(In this sentence, the subject is *children*, which is plural; therefore, it agrees with *watch*, the main verb.)

The *child*, whenever she is with her father, *watches* television.
(Singular subject agrees with verb with -*s* ending.)

This rule also applies to the auxiliaries *is* and *was* and *has* in the continuous tenses of the present and past, and the present perfect tense. (For more on this subject, refer to Section IX. *Verbs* in this Appendix.)

B. Read the following student essay. As you read, look for subject-verb agreement errors.

Literacy Issues in the United States

1 There is a lack of reading in every home in the United States of America. The president of this country have addressed this issue several times. Who is to blame for this lack of reading? Parents, kids, the educational system or the government?

2 The president put the blame on parents. The truth is that getting our kids to pick up a book sometimes appear impossible.

3 We, the parents, should also think hard about the example we sets for our children. If parents comes home from work and sits in front of the television set to relax, that won't inspire kids to see reading as pleasurable relaxation. They will only emulate their parents.

4 The educational system are to blame also for our kids' lack of desire to read. Students rarely reads any thing at school besides their textbooks. From kindergarten through the 12th grade, children should spend at least eighteen hours per week devoted to reading books other than texts. This might be due to the great amount of material modern schools have to teach. There seem not to be enough time in schools for reading for curiosity, least of all reading for pleasure.

5 Then, the president, as a representative of the government, are partly to blame. To mention the problem in his speeches is not the only solution. The president is in power to do more for the problem. Instead we see government which does not prioritize the needs of children or their education. For example, there are fewer teachers in our city schools than there was years ago. The reason for these cuts are the depletion of the U. S. Treasury. Nevertheless, budget cuts is not the solution; that only increases the problem. The president should reassign moneys that is used for defense in order to reinforce education, and redesign the curriculum of schools to make learning (and reading) fun.

Go back to the beginning of the essay. Carefully read each sentence. Circle errors in subject-verb agreement. Rewrite the sentences, correcting the subject-verb agreement errors.

C. Now look at your own draft that you are revising. Correct any similar errors.

III. Adjectives

A. As you know, adjectives are modifiers; they modify (or describe) nouns and pronouns. If a word is modifying a noun or a pronoun, you know it is an adjective. (If it is modifying a verb, or if it is modifying another modifier, then it is an adverb.)

- Adjectives answer questions about the nouns, such as which one? how many? what kind? For example:

  the *tall* dinosaur

  the *only* hope

  the *seven* sons

- Adjectives usually appear before the noun in English. (This is often *not* the case in other languages.)

- Very often you will see more than one adjective in front of a noun in English. This is acceptable. Usually a series of adjectives will be separated by commas. For example:

  The *two tall, beautiful, yellow* birds made strange noises.

- Adjectives may be changed to show degrees of comparison.

quick	quicker	quickest
young	younger	youngest

- The *-er* ending is called the *comparative* form. Use this when you are showing the difference between two things. For example:

  She is a *slower* swimmer than he is.

- The *-est* ending is called the superlative form. Use this when you are showing the difference among more than two things. For example:

  She is the *slowest* swimmer on the whole team.

- The use of *-er* at the end of an adjective is similar to using the intensifier *more* in front of the adjective. The use of *-est* at the end of the adjective is similar to using the intensifier *most* in front of the adjective. For example:

  She is *more intelligent* than he is.

  She is the *most intelligent* student in the class.

In general, when the adjective has more than two syllables, *more* and *most* are used; when the adjective has one or two syllables, the *-er* and *-est* endings are used.

more interesting	most interesting
(NOT *interestinger*)	(NOT *interestingest*)

B. Read the following student essay. As you read, look for errors involving adjective usage.

The Problem of Crime in Large Cities

1 The problem of crime is one of more bigger problems in large cities like New York, where I live. New York is a city where the sophisticateder people, the people who have money, live. Others, who do not have money see these more rich people and their life style and feel envious.

2 In addition, there are people who cannot find a job. Then they have nothing to do, so they become more lazy and more angriest. When they cannot find money with legal means, they become criminals. When police catch them, they do not stay in jail longer; soon they are more wild and more destructiver than they were before.

3 In my country, there is an efficienter criminal justice system. If a person is found guilty, he does not go free soon; he is put behind bars for a more long time than in the United States. Sometimes people can be in jail for longest than thirty years. When they finally leave the prison, they are honester people.

4 Two things could be done to improve life and get rid of crime. First, make opportunities more better so that people can find work, and stay off the street. Then, provide a gooder criminal justice system, where the guilty are properly punished.

Go back to the beginning of the essay. Carefully read each sentence. Circle errors in adjective use. Rewrite the sentences, correcting the adjective errors.

C. Now, look at your own draft. Do you have any errors involving adjectives?

IV. Relative Clauses

A. Look at the following sentence.

The dog, which was in the pet shop, was asleep.

Notice that the words

which was in the pet shop

tell *which* dog. In other words, they modify that noun.

In that example, *which was in the pet shop* is an *adjective relative clause*, because it behaves like an adjective by modifying the noun *dog*.

A clause is a group of words which, like a sentence, has a subject and a verb. In this case, the subject of the relative clause is the relative pronoun, *which*. *Which*, in this case, is substituting for *dog*. The original sentence could actually be broken down into two very simple sentences:

The dog was asleep.

+

The dog was in the pet shop.

When you combine them, you substitute the relative pronoun *which* instead of repeating *dog* a second time. Thus,

The dog, which was in the pet shop, was asleep.

Other relative pronouns that can be used to replace a noun in this type of sentence are

who	whom
whose	that

- Sometimes, *when, where,* and *why* are used to introduce a relative clause.
  - I remember the time *when* we were young.
  - This is the place *where* the man was injured.
- Humans are referred to with *who, whose,* and *whom.*
  - The man *who* wore a red coat was on the subway.

  Who is in the subject position.
  - The man to *whom* they were calling turned around.

  Whom is in the object position.
  - This is the man *whose* hat we found.

  Whose is in the adjective position.

While *who* refers only to humans, *that* and *which* can in some cases refer to humans, but more often refer to nouns other than humans.

He took the paper *that* was in his mailbox.

B. Read the following student essay. Try to find errors with relative clauses.

Keeping Informed

1 One of the greatest things in the world is the modern media and communication systems. The majority of the people around the world. That like to be informed listen to the news. Incredible events are often happening every day in science, politics, society, or sports events. News can be transmitted by radio, the newspapers, and television. Who in a matter of minutes can take information from one side of the globe to the other.

2 When we watch the news on television, we can see events who are instantaneously happening as if we were on the scene at the time. We can see the event who as it unfolds in some exotic spot on the globe. An example is the inquisition of Supreme Court nominee Clarence Thomas, whose was accused by Anita Hill of sexual harassment. That drama on television helped us understand what really goes on in Washington. Those proceedings made history. Another point is listening to the radio news can make us feel the excitement or the sadness whom is in the narrator's voice. Public radio can give us an unbiased view of major world situations.

3 Getting informed through the newspaper is the most common way who the everyday working class person can get information. In addition, newspapers and journals which can give us photos and pictures to help us visualize the events reported. In summary, there is no excuse for any individual which can see or hear to miss important happenings on this planet.

Go back over the essay and circle the mistakes. Correct the relative clause errors.

C. Can you find similar mistakes in any of your drafts? Compare your draft with mistakes cited in the preceding essay.

V. Infinitives and Gerunds

A. *Infinitives* and *gerunds* are verb formations in which the verb is used as a noun. You are already familiar with verbs as the action, state of being, or linking word in a sentence.

We *read* books every day.

- If you take a verb (such as *read*) and put *to* in front of it, you create a form called the *infinitive.*

  To read is an important first step in order to revise.

  The infinitive *to read* is the subject of the sentence. In this case, then, the infinitive clearly acts like a noun.

- Sometimes, an infinitive takes an object; at other times, it is part of a clause. Look at the two following sentences.

  He asked Susanna *to read* the essay aloud.
  He wanted *to read* the essay aloud.

  Compare the two sentences. What is the difference? In the first, *Susanna to read the essay* is the object of the verb *asked*. In the second sentence, the object is *the essay*.

- Some verbs cannot be followed by a noun and an infinitive. Those verbs are: *hope, decide, agree, refuse,* and *appear*.

- A *gerund* is the verb + *-ing* suffix. Gerunds, like infinitives, can work as nouns.

  Studying is difficult in May and June.
  Studying English is difficult in May and June.

  In the two preceding sentences, the gerund *studying* is a noun. Note that it is acting in the role of the subject, just as the infinitive did in an earlier example. Note also that, in the second sentence, *studying* has an object: *English.* In the first sentence, there is no object of the gerund. Gerunds can function with or without objects in different situations.

- Also like infinitives, gerunds can be in the object position.

  He hated *answering* in front of the whole class.
  She listed *running* as a hobby she enjoyed.

B. Carefully read the following student essay. Circle each error and analyze it. All errors will involve the formation of gerunds and infinitives.

Sexual Harassment on the Job

1 Sexual harassment has become a major issue since the Women's Liberation Movement started take place in the late 60s and early 70s. There are numerous places and occasions where sexual harassment incidents are continuing happen. This time we will discuss sexual harassment in the job scene. We will talk about society's pressure and the injustices by the act to commit discrimination.

2 We learn that many of the sexual harassment incidents have been reported as occur on the job. For example, offer secretaries a better position in exchange for sexual favors is a common situation in business. Although to give in is not the answer, these individuals leave the position and report it many years later they have left the job. Many of these people, like Anita Hill, do not want taking a strong stand in court because they do not want suffer the consequences professionally.

3 In spite of many recent gains in women's rights, women and minorities still have a long way go.

Now, rewrite the sentences where there are mistakes with gerunds or infinitives.

C. Look at your draft to find mistakes that are similar. Check to see if you used any gerunds or infinitives. If not, substitute them in the place of some nouns.

VI. Prepositions

A. ESL students sometimes find English prepositions to be challenging. Some of the most common ones are:

at	*At* the stroke of midnight, the door opened. She met me *at* the candy store.
by	The scuba equipment was used *by* Cousteau. Be home *by* 9:00.
in	He went to the dance *in* an old car. The teacher is *in* her office.
from	The letter was *from* the doctor. Hitomi ran *from* the car to the house.

of	Annette is the president *of* the student body. This is the longest night *of* the year.
for	The telephone call was *for* you. She worked hard *for* a raise.
on	Marie lived *on* 23rd Street. My father has no hair *on* his head.
to	The rebels sent the telegram *to* Port-au-Prince. Santa Claus came *to* our house this year.
with	The dog played *with* the dead rat. Charles made bacon *with* eggs.
until	The party lasted *until* dawn. We wrote *until* the teacher told us to stop.
into	The people went *into* the cave to live for two years. Five goes *into* 100 twenty times.

Look up the preceding prepositions in the dictionary. You will notice some have more than one meaning.

- Prepositions are used to establish relationships with time and space, and relationships between people or animals and objects.

  Some meanings of prepositions are idiomatic in English, and have to be memorized. Here are some examples:

  - *At* + time:

    I will be waiting for you *at two o'cloc*k.

  - *At* + place:

    At the movies I saw the professor.

  - *At* + address

    Keiko lives *at 456 Park Avenue.*

  - *In* + geographical location:

    She lives *in New York*, but for years she lived *in Spain.*

B. Read the following student essay. Circle the sentences that have preposition errors.

Immigrants' Experience: Across Cultures

1 It was 1967 when my family moved at Puerto Rico. They had finally bought their dream house on a town called Carolina. Moving to Puerto Rico was a total change for my mother, who was born and raised at Philadelphia. When she was eighteen years old, she moved into New York City, where she met my father, Jose.

2 Several years later, they got married. Both worked very hard. They saved all the money they could for accomplish their goal for buy a house in the beautiful island of Puerto Rico, where my father had lived on his youth.

3 I was the first born for four children. I was four years old when we moved. My father had obtained a job at the Hotel San Juan, which was one of the most beautiful tourist areas for Isla Verde. This was three miles away near home. Meanwhile, my mother took care of my sister and me. Whenever she went out, she would take us with her, mostly for the supermarket or for the park.

4 As time went by, we had gotten more familiar on the neighborhood. Also we had started to meet some the people who were nearby. For many of our neighbors, my mother and I were a novelty for it was not common to see people in an Anglo appearance. My mother was fairly tall as comparison with the average Puerto Rican. She was also very blonde. Every time we passed by a group of people, someone would say, "Ahi va la Gringa!" (There goes the American lady!)

5 Today, more than 20 years have passed since she moved at the island of Puerto Rico. She has even learned to cook the traditional arroz con habichuelas. Although she initially had some culture shock, especially for learning the language, she has developed great love after the island and its people.

Read the preceding composition once again. Circle the errors made with prepositions. Write the correct form of the preposition.

C. Look in your own draft to see if you have similar errors involving prepositions.

VII. Punctuation: Fragments and Run-Ons

A. As we discussed in Chapter 1, every English sentence must have a subject and a verb. It must also "sound complete"; that is, it must express a complete idea, and not sound like something is missing. If it sounds incomplete, it is a fragment.

Because revising is hard work.

This sentence does not "sound complete" because it begins with *because. Because* always introduces a dependent adverb clause. A dependent clause cannot stand alone as a sentence; by itself, it is only a fragment.

As a fragment—not a sentence—it should not be punctuated as a sentence.

Other words that begin dependent adverb clauses are:

after	We met the band *after the concert ended.*
when	*When we ran out of money*, we panicked.
although	*Although Linda can be nice*, she's often cranky.
before	*Before we had children*, we could go out at night.
as	We took the plane to the island *as the hurricane struck the mainland.*
since	*Since the video store opened in the neighborhood*, the kids all hang out there.

Another punctuation error committed frequently is joining two complete sentences with a comma. This creates a run-on.

Revising is hard work even when you are a published author, if you do not revise you will eventually be sorry.

Writing is like thinking on paper, your thoughts are put in concrete form so that you can analyze them and change them.

In each of the above sentences, you need to use a period instead of a comma. Each of these examples should be two sentences, not one run-on.

B. Read the following student essay. Look for fragments and run-on sentences.

Abortion

1 Abortion is a controversial issue in the United States. Because religion comes into the question. People differ in their opinions about abortion, for many years the issue has been discussed on television, in magazines, and in the newspapers. The issue is whether women have the right to control their own bodies, or whether the government can make it illegal.

2 I disagree that women should be told what to do by the government, they should have the right to make their own decisions. Since it is their body. However this is a complicated issue because it is wrong to use abortion as a method of birth control. If a woman has been irresponsible and has become pregnant. She should not have an abortion just to kill the fetus. On the other hand there are tragedies like when a teenager is raped, there should be a way of solving this by an abortion early in the pregnancy, the other crime is incest, the victim should not have to pay for the violation against them.

3 Another situation that comes to mind is. When the mother's life is in danger. In this case, like the ones preceding, an abortion can be justified, however not just to solve a problem of indiscretion quickly. For this we have to address the moral issues of our society. Because we are setting the stage for the next generation. When the future citizens are born. They will inherit a moral, humane world or an immoral one.

Correct the mistakes with punctuation in the preceding essay.

C. Look for similar mistakes in your own compositions. Correct mistakes made with punctuation by looking to see if every sentence is a complete unit and has a subject and a verb.

VIII. Modals

A. Modals are auxiliaries which go with the main verb, and which carry meaning. You will often find them useful in argument writing.

Here are the most common modals.

- You *should* eat fruits and vegetables.

Should implies advice.

- Students *should* respect their teachers.

Should implies obligation.

• You *ought to* clean your room.
Ought to implies obligation.

• If you do not want to get hurt, you *must* obey the traffic light.
Must implies necessity.

• You *must not* eat poison.
Must not implies a prohibition.

• Sarah's teacher says she *has to* do her homework on time.
Has to implies necessity.

• This activity is extra. You do *not have to* do it if you do not want to.
Not have to implies not necessary.

• She *can* make A's if she really tries.
Can implies able to.

• *Can* I leave now?
Can implies permission.

• He *could* win the game if he were ready to play.
Could implies possibility in the present tense.

• *Could* I have a conference with you this afternoon?
Could implies permission.

• *May* I have the honor of this dance?
May implies permission and is more polite than *can* or *could.*

• The bird *may* fly if you startle it.
May implies probability.

• She *might* go home, or she *might* go to the movies.
Might implies probability.

B. Read the following student essay carefully to see if there are mistakes made with modals. Circle the sentences where the mistakes occur.

Preventing Home Accidents

1 Home accidents can often be caused by children who live in homes where there is no appropriate supervision by an adult. As adults, we may take care of our children wherever they are. As

parents, we could follow some important rules for our children so that they might suffer accidents in their own home.

2 Someone must always clean the floor and keep out of reach sharp objects such as pins and needles because our children have to hurt their feet. Another rule that is going to prevent a fatal accident is to cover electric outlets that children can could not put things into them such as pins and must not get electric shocks which may ought to harm them. Also, children may could put matches in their mouths, or start fires with them, so they can put out of sight.

3 Our children may be safe from accidents if we take good care of them and make sure the environment where they live is a safe one. We can not prevent accidents if we love our children.

Go back to the beginning of the essay and reread it. Circle the mistakes made with modals. Now rewrite the sentences using modals correctly.

C. Search your draft for similar mistakes with modals. Make sure you understand the meanings of modals. Some have similar meanings, others are quite different. Refer to the list above.

IX. Verbs

A. In Chapter 5, you edited your drafts for inconsistencies in tense. Here is more information about the English verb tense system.

- The *Simple Present* describes actions that are repeated, or habitual. This tense is sometimes called "the descriptive present" because it is used to describe persons, places, or things.

  I *walk* to the college every day.
  The college *sits* on a hill.

- The *Present Continuous* is often called the "true present" because it is used to denote action that is taking place *now*, in the immediate present.

  I *am typing* on the computer right now.

- The *Simple Past* is used to describe past action that took place at a definite time in the past.

  Yesterday I *walked* to the college in a hail storm.

- The *Past Continuous* is used to describe past action that has continued for a period of time in the past.

  I *was commuting* an hour and a half to work every day for a year.

- The *Simple Future* is used to describe action that will take place in the future.

  I *will walk* to the college next Monday to attend class.

- The *Future Continuous* is used to describe future actions that will go on for a time.

  I *will be walking* to class for the remainder of the semester.

- The *Present Perfect* is used to describe past action that began in the past at a specific time.

  I *have walked* to class many times in the snow.

- The *Present Perfect Continuous* shows action that began at a time in the past and has continued until the present time.

  I *have been walking* two miles a day for two years.

- The *Past Perfect* is used to describe past action that began at a point in the past and continued until a designated time in the past.

  I *had walked* to the student union when the clock began to chime.

- The *Past Perfect Continuous* shows past action that began in the past and continued for a time.

  I *had been walking* for an hour when I developed a cramp in my leg.

- The *Future Perfect* is used to describe an action that will occur up until a designated time in the future.

  I *will have walked* a mile a day for two years by next June.

- The *Future Perfect Continuous* is used to designate an action that will have been taking place up to the time of another action in the future.

  I *will have been walking* two miles a day for ten years by next June.

You will probably not use all of the tenses above often. You will sometimes see them in your reading.

B. In the following student essay, try to recognize incorrect uses of tense. Circle the incorrect sentences.

Gun Control

1 In today's society, the issue of gun control had become an important issue. Each minute, more and more people were becoming affected by guns. People are being killed by random violence involving guns. Old people and children were often victims of an armed criminal's shots.

2 A woman, Yu-an Li, lives in my neighborhood where she is teaches piano. She was walking home from the corner grocery store when this man carrying a gun will shooting a shopkeeper after an attempted robbery. One of the stray bullets is hitting her and she died. Now her daughters were sad because the man had not been caught by the police and was still free in the streets with his gun.

3 In the past few months, the federal government were debated this issue and are attempting to pass a law requiring a waiting period so that the store owner had checked the buyer for a possible criminal record before purchasing a gun. Furthermore, the National Rifle Association will be fighting last fall to have this law stopped. They feel that it is an infringement on their constitutional rights. How many people die before something is done?

Now reread the essay to find errors in verb tense. Remember, there should not be a change of tense when there is no urgent reason for it.

C. Look in your own draft to see if you can find similar errors in verb tenses.

▶Appendix 2: Irregular Verbs

Base form	Past form	Participle form
arise	arose	arisen
awake	awoke / awaked	awoke / awaked
be	was	been
beat	beat	beaten
become	became	become
begin	began	begun
bend	bent	bent
bet	bet	bet
bite	bit	bitten
bleed	bled	bled
blow	blew	blown
break	broke	broken
bring	brought	brought
build	built	built
burn	burned	burnt
buy	bought	bought
catch	caught	caught
choose	chose	chosen
come	came	come
cost	cost	cost
cut	cut	cut
deal	dealt	dealt
do	did	done
draw	drew	drawn
dream	dreamt / dreamed	dreamt / dreamed
drink	drank	drunk
drive	drove	driven

Base form	Past form	Participle form
eat	ate	eaten
fall	fell	fallen
feed	fed	fed
feel	felt	felt
fight	fought	fought
find	found	found
fly	flew	flown
forget	forgot	forgotten
forgive	forgave	forgiven
freeze	froze	frozen
get	got	gotten
give	gave	given
go	went	gone
grow	grew	grown
hang	hung	hanged
have	had	had
hear	heard	heard
hide	hid	hidden
hit	hit	hit
hold	held	held
hurt	hurt	hurt
keep	kept	kept
know	knew	known
lay	laid	laid
lead	led	led
lean	leaned	leaned
leave	left	left
lend	lent	lent
let	let	let
lie	lay	lain

Base form	Past form	Participle form
light	lit	lit
lose	lost	lost
make	made	made
mean	meant	meant
meet	met	met
pay	paid	paid
prove	proved	proven
put	put	put
read	read	read
ride	rode	ridden
ring	rang	rung
rise	rose	risen
run	ran	run
say	said	said
see	saw	seen
sell	sold	sold
send	sent	sent
set	set	set
sew	sewed	sewn
shake	shook	shaken
shave	shaved	shaved / shaven
shine	shone	shined
shoot	shot	shot
show	showed	shown
shut	shut	shut
sing	sang	sung
sit	sat	sat
sleep	slept	slept
speak	spoke	spoken
spend	spent	spent

Base form	Past form	Participle form
stand	stood	stood
steal	stole	stolen
stick	stuck	stuck
swim	swam	swum
take	took	taken
teach	taught	taught
tear	tore	torn
tell	told	told
think	thought	thought
throw	threw	thrown
understand	understood	understood
wake	woke / waked	woken / waked
wear	wore	worn
weep	wept	wept
win	won	won
wind	wound	wound
withdraw	withdrew	withdrawn
write	wrote	written

GLOSSARY

Each of the words in this Glossary is highlighted in one of the reading selections in this book. The number of the chapter in which the word is first used is indicated in parentheses.

While many words can have several alternative definitions, and most words can be used as several different parts of speech depending upon the context, the definitions and the part of speech designation given in the Glossary correspond to the way the word is used in the reading selection.

Abbreviations:

n. noun
v. verb
adj. adjective
adv. adverb

acid runoff (6) n., toxic liquid residue that leeches into the drinking water supply

adamantly (2) adv., strongly; vehemently

advocate (3) n., a person who speaks for or supports an idea; v., to speak for an idea

alteration (6) n., a change

ambivalence (4) n., a sense of having opposing feelings; indecision

ample (3) adj., plentiful; available in large quantity

anathema (7) n., something hated

appalling (2) adj., horrifying; saddening

array (6) n., assortment; a range

assessment (3) n., evaluation; measurement

assurance (3) n., the state of feeling certain; a promise

at stake (3) adj., at risk

aura (4) n., an effect that seems to surround or emanate weirdly from someone or something; a surrounding glow

aversion (6) n., a strong dislike
awesome (3) adj., inspiring awe; majestic
betrayal (3) n., an act of disloyalty or unfaithfulness
bigots (7) n., a prejudiced individual; a racist
budged (4) v., moved slightly
carnage (2) n., bloodshed; the aftermath of a violent act
catastrophe (6) n., disaster
cloning (5) n., non-sexual reproduction of identical offspring of plants or animals from a single cell of the "parent"
coercion (5) n., the act of forcing someone to act or think in a given manner
compliance (3) n., agreement; cooperation
compress (3) v., squeeze together; confine to a smaller than usual area to make smaller
consensus (5) n., agreement
contemplative (5) adj., thoughtful; meditative
contentious (6) adj., argumentative
contrition (3) n., guilt; penitence
correlation (3) n., a shared, connected, or causal relationship
crucial (2) adj., of the greatest importance
data (3) n., information
debunking (2) v., pointing out the falseness of a wrong idea
dehydration (5) n., the act of drying or removing all the water from something
demeaning (5) adj., humiliating
demographic (4) adj., pertaining to population
deterrent (2) n., something that prevents (or attempts to prevent) an action
detrimental (3) adj., destructive; harmful
dichotomy (4) n., something that has two parts
disenfranchised (1) adj., made weak or powerless
dumpster (1) n., a large canister into which garbage cans are emptied
elusive (4) adj., hard to pin down
embryo (5) n., the first stage of development of any organism
endorsed (3) v., supported; expressed approval of publicly
entitled (3) adj., deserving of something

epidemic (2) n., a rapidly spreading disease, such as a flu epidemic or the AIDS epidemic; figuratively, a spreading or growing problem

episodic (6) adj., something occurring as a separate event

erosion (2) n., a wearing away

escalation (2) n., an increase; especially a rapid increase

excised (7) v., removed

extinct (5) adj., no longer existing in living form

fanaticism (5) n., a strong belief that does not allow the believer to consider any other point of view; extremism

federal legislation (2) n., national law

felons (2) n., criminals

fetus (5) n., the later stage of development of certain animals within the womb (in a human, beginning after the 8th week after conception)

firearms (2) n., guns

flagrant (7) adj., blatant; conspicuous

fostered (2) v., made easier

fundamental (2) adj., basic; vital

geneticist (4) n., a scientist who studies heredity

genocide (5) n., the systematic, planned annihilation of a racial, political, or cultural group

gestation (5) n., the period of carrying developing offspring in a mother's womb; pregnancy

grapple (4) v., wrestle; struggle

gratified (2) v., satisfied; appeased

grievance (3) n., complaint

goundwater (6) n., water beneath the earth's surface that supplies wells and springs

guise (3) n., disguise; costume

hallmark (5) n., any indication of quality or excellence

hamper (4) v., to block or get in the way of something; to impede progress

harass (2) v., annoy; persecute

heinous (2) v., abominable; inhuman; monstrous

herbicides (6) v., chemicals used to kill weeds or other unwanted plant growth

impede (3) v., to slow something down; to get in the way of someone's (or something's) progress
implement (3) v., achieve; fulfill
importation (2) n., the act of purchasing and bringing goods into a country from another country, for resale
imprecations (1) n., curses
inanimate (2) adj., not alive; not able to move on its own
incarcerate (2) v., to imprison
inequities (3) n., inequalities; differences (often, unfair or prejudicial differences)
inherent (2) adj., intrinsic; inborn
initiated (2) v., began
initiative (4) n., an enterprise or a program
innate (4) adj., possessed at birth; inborn
interdependent (3) adj., mutually dependent
intrinsic (3) adj., natural; indigenous
intuitive (4) adj., based on feelings or guesses, as opposed to reason or logic
invective (7) n., sharp, harsh, insulting words used to attack
invoked (6) v., called upon a higher power
legacy (2) n., something passed on or left behind, as an inheritance
libel (7) n., the making of a written statement that damages someone's reputation
linguist (3) n., someone who studies the science of language
lucrative (4) adj., highly profitable
magnitude (6) n., greatness of size or importance
marksmanship (2) n., ability to hit a target with a gun
massacre (2) n., the act of killing a large number of victims
mastery (3) n., control over or skill in
medium (3) n., means; vehicle
merge (3) v., to go together and become one
metaphor (3) n., a figurative use of language in which something is described by comparing it with another thing
mindset (6) n., a fixed perspective; a mental approach
mired (4) adj., stuck
miscarriage (5) n., the early, involuntary expulsion of a nonviable fetus in mid-pregnancy
mute (3) adj., silent

mythic (3) adj., not real; imagined or invented
near-term (5) adj., at a time close to being born; near the end of gestation
nurture (3) v., care for; nourish; parent
oracles (2) n., ones who predict the future
ordain (5) v., decree; legislate
outrage (2) n., anger; shock
overhaul (4) v., to completely redo or reconstruct
oversee (1) v., to be responsible for
parable (3) n., story with symbolic significance
paradox (3) n., a seeming impossibility; contradiction
partisans (5) n., holders of a particular opinion in a controversy
passersby (1) n., those who happen by chance to be near an event (such as a crime)
pelts (5) n., animal skins
pending (4) adj., waiting; soon to be acted upon
pesticides (6) n., chemicals used on crops to kill unwanted insects
piecemeal (4) adj., one at a time
pinnacle (4) n., peak
poised (2) adj., ready
policy (1) n., procedure; practice
practicably (7) adv., with practicality; in a useable manner
precepts (7) n., rules; tenets
predecessors (4) n., those who came before; ancestors
prerequisites (3) n., prior requirements; things needed before one can proceed
proficient (3) adj., capable
prohibitionists (2) n., those in favor of making something illegal
punitive (4) adj., designed to inflict punishment
recruiter (4) n., a person whose job it is to seek new employees
relinquish (3) v., let something go
retreat (3) v., the act of going back, withdrawing
retrenchment (3) n., pulling back; the act of reorganizing something and making it smaller or more conservative
rhetorical (3) adj., used in language only for effect
roving (1) v., moving around
scheme (3) n., plan

scrupulously (5) adv., carefully
shelters (1) n., buildings or enclosures used for basic protection
short-lived (6) adj., not living or lasting long
slanders (7) n., insults; defamations
span (2) v., to cross or bridge
specter (5) n., a frightening image
spit out (1) v., emit; eject
stabilized (2) v., made steady or regular
statistical (3) adj., of the mathematics of the organization of numerical data
steadfastly (2) adv., faithfully; loyally
subsequent (3) adj., following
supplement (3) n., a part added to a newspaper or magazine
tabulated (5) v., calculated using numbers; counted
tantamount (5) adj., equal in value, force, or effect
testimony (2) n., a sworn statement, given under oath (as in a trial or a government hearing, for example)
thermal (6) adj., of, using, or producing heat
toxic (6) adj., poisonous
trainees (2) n., people who are learning, such as new employees
trendy (2) adj., stylish; currently popular
triage (6) n., the process of deciding among many patients the order in which those patients should be treated
vermillion (1) n., bright red color
waive (2) v., put aside
writhing (5) v., twisting or contorting
yearn (3) v., to strongly desire

INDEX

CREDITS

▶Text

We would like to thank the authors, publishers, and holders of copyright for use of the following material.

The New York Times:

"Public & Private, Rooms of Their Own," Anna Quindlen, Jan. 21, 1990. Copyright © 1990 The New York Times Company. Reprinted by permission.

"Bilingualism, Pro: The Key to Basic Skills, Native Language Held Vital to Self-Esteem and Motivation," Angelo Gonzalez, Nov. 10, 1985. Copyright © 1985 by The New York Times Company. Reprinted by permission.

"Bilingualism, Con: Outdated and Unrealistic," Richard Rodriguez, Nov. 10, 1985. Copyright © 1985 by The New York Times Company. Reprinted by permission.

"Bilingualism's Goal," Barbara Mujica, Feb. 26, 1984. Copyright © 1984 by The New York Times Company. Reprinted by permission.

"What Really Threatens the Environment?" William K. Stevens, Jan. 29, 1991. Copyright © 1991 by The New York Times Company. Reprinted by permission.

"Student at Brown Is Expelled Under a Rule Barring 'Hate Speech'," Feb. 12, 1991.

"How Much Hate to Tolerate," [editorial] Feb. 21, 1991.

"Brown Expulsion Not About Free Speech," Vartan Gregorian, Feb. 21, 1991.

[letter] copyrighted by Harvard Hollenberg, 1991, and used with permission. All rights to the content and manner of expression, as well as to the text, remain in and with Harvard Hollenberg, including but not limited to media and fiction use.

[letter] Hyman H. Haves, March 16, 1991

[letter] Nadine Strosser, March 16, 1991

Time Inc. Magazine (Copyright 1990 The Time Inc. Company. Reprinted by permission.):

"The Case for Firearms . . . " J. Warren Cassidy, Jan. 29, 1990.

". . . And the Case Against Them," Sarah Brady, Jan. 29, 1990.

U. S. News & World Report:

"Trouble at the Top," Amy Saltzman, Copyright June 17, 1991.

Parade Publications, Inc.:

"Is It Possible to Be Pro-Life *and* Pro-Choice?" Carl Sagan and Ann Druyan, April 22, 1990.

▶Photos

Ann Marie Rousseau/Image Works, p. 1.

The Rio, fifth in a series of buildings in Washington Heights restored under the supervision of Ellen Baxter. Photo courtesy of Community Service Society of New York, p. 15.

George Gardner/Image Works, p. 17.

Seconds before the assassination attempt on President Reagan. Jim Brady is the third person from the left. UPI/Bettmann, p. 34.

Bob Daemmrich/Image Works, p. 35.

Jonathan A. Meyers/FPG, p. 57.

Elizabeth Crews/Image Works, p. 59.

Jim Pickerell/Image Works, p. 75.

Bob Daemmrich/Image Works, p. 77.

Hamster sperm and egg at moment of conception. David Phillips/Photo Researchers, p. 91.

Charles Gatewood/Image Works, p. 93.

Linda Watkins-Goffman and Richard Goffman investigating life in the ocean, p. 108.

John Forasté/Brown University, p. 109.